Good Housekeeping

light & healthy
COOKING

More than 125 Delicious, Satisfying, Guilt-Free Recipes

Shrimp Kabobs with Asian BBQ Sauce (recipe page 74)

Good Housekeeping

light & healthy
COOKING

More than 125 Delicious, Satisfying, Guilt-Free Recipes

HEARST BOOKS
New York

HEARST BOOKS
New York

An Imprint of Sterling Publishing
387 Park Avenue South
New York, NY 10016

GOOD HOUSEKEEPING

Rosemary Ellis	*Editor in Chief*
Courtney Murphy	*Creative Director*
Susan Westmoreland	*Food Director*
Samantha B. Cassetty, MS, RD	*Nutrition Director*

Book Design: Anna Christian
Cover Design: Jon Chaiet
Project Editor: Sarah Scheffel

Photography Credits on page 137

KOHL'S
ISBN 978-1-61837-081-5
Factory Number: 123386
10/12

This special edition was printed for Kohl's Department Stores, Inc. (for distribution on behalf of Kohl's Cares, LLC, its wholly owned subsidiary) by Hearst Books, a division of Sterling Publishing Co., Inc.

10 9 8 7 6 5 4 3 2 1

The Good Housekeeping Cookbook Seal guarantees that the recipes in this cookbook meet the strict standards of the Good Housekeeping Research Institute. The Institute has been a source of reliable information and a consumer advocate since 1900, and established its seal of approval in 1909. Every recipe has been triple-tested for ease, reliability, and great taste.

Published by Hearst Books
A division of Sterling Publishing Co., Inc.
387 Park Avenue South, New York, NY 10016

Good Housekeeping is a registered trademark of Hearst Communications, Inc.
www.goodhousekeeping.com

For information about custom editions, special sales, premium and corporate purchases, please contact Sterling Special Sales Department at 800-805-5489 or specialsales@sterlingpublishing.com.

Distributed in Canada by Sterling Publishing
c/o Canadian Manda Group, 165 Dufferin Street
Toronto, Ontario, Canada M6K 3H6

Distributed in Australia by Capricorn Link (Australia) Pty. Ltd.
P.O. Box 704, Windsor, NSW 2756 Australia

Manufactured in China

Sterling ISBN 978-1-61837-081-5

Basil-Orange Chicken with Couscous (recipe page 89)

Orange Pork and Asparagus Stir-Fry (recipe page 108)

Contents

Honeyed Hot Fruit Salad (recipe page 134)

Foreword

Welcome to *Good Housekeeping*'s collection of our favorite light and healthy recipes.

We all want to eat nutritious meals. But sometimes it's hard finding easy, healthy recipes that everyone in your family will love. That's why we're so pleased to present this cookbook. Not only did we fill it with delicious recipes your family will want to eat, we created many dishes that are ready in less than 30 minutes to please the cook, too. Icons throughout the book indicate these quick-and-easy dishes, plus high-fiber, heart-healthy, and make-ahead options. (See Index of Recipes by Icon, page 142, for a complete list.)

The more than 125 breakfasts, salads, soups, sandwiches, main dishes, and sides in this book are sure crowd pleasers, whether you're making Tuesday night family dinner or entertaining a group of friends on the weekend. Each recipe has been triple-tested by the pros in the *Good Housekeeping* Test Kitchens, so you can be sure they'll come out great. Many feature whole grains, which fill you up with wholesome fiber and other essential nutrients, too.

In every recipe, 30 percent or fewer of the calories come from fat. That's right in line with the USDA's dietary guidelines for healthy eating. We also offer info about healthy ingredients to include in your diet, plus cooking tips from our expert team to help make your everyday food preparation as easy and healthy as can be!

You'll quickly discover that cooking with an eye toward good health doesn't mean sacrificing taste or familiar foods you know your family will eat. Stir fries, pastas, fajitas, burgers, and even mashed potatoes and fries? Yes, all of these can be light and nutritious.

Here's to happy, healthy cooking for you and your family!

—Susan Westmoreland
Food Director, *Good Housekeeping*

Eating Well, the Light and Healthy Way

Providing healthy, low-calorie (not to mention low-fat) meals that are satisfying and easy to prepare is a big concern for all of us today. As the relationship between diet and health hits the headlines repeatedly, we all want to do our best to produce meals for our families and ourselves that meet today's nutritional guidelines. But figuring out how to do it isn't always easy. The latest USDA Dietary Guidelines (healthierus .gov/dietaryguidelines) and Choose My Plate

(ChooseMyPlate.gov) have revised the rules based on current medical research, but the goal is the same: to encourage us all to eat a diet that will lead to a long life of good health.

Over the years, *Good Housekeeping* has been a trusted source for making the latest information on health and nutrition a part of your daily life. As the rules change, *Good Housekeeping* editors translate the underlying research and provide the tools you need to make it work for you. Our *Light & Healthy Cooking* follows that tradition by bringing you this collection of delicious, triple-tested recipes that meet the latest USDA dietary guidelines. The recipes selected emphasize whole grains, an abundance of fruits and vegetables, and fat-free or low-fat dairy products. They include fish, lean poultry, and meat, as well as beans, eggs, and nuts, but limit total fat to 30 percent of calories or less (the USDA cap is 35 percent), and also saturated fat, trans fat, cholesterol, and added sugar. Recipes keep tabs on sodium, too.

Calories Count

We hear a lot about America's obesity epidemic and the "flavor-of-the-day" diets that everyone is trying—but very little about counting calories. Calories aren't an old-fashioned enemy; they are simply a way of measuring the amount of energy produced when food is used by the body. Keeping an eye on them is still the most promising method to ease into a lifetime of weight control. In fact, one of the USDA's key recommendations is to manage body weight by controlling total calorie intake. It's just a matter of balance: Food calories in must equal energy calories out. For people who are overweight or obese, this will mean consuming fewer calories and increasing physical activity.

For centuries, our bodies have been stocking up during times of plenty to insure survival during times of scarcity, so we are naturally programmed to tuck away all excess food calories as those potential energy calories we know as fat. And that is not likely to change any time soon. You might try the latest diet fad and enjoy short-term success, but pretty soon your body will think the famine it has been planning for has arrived and will steadfastly hang on to those stored calories in case things get worse.

When it comes to light and healthy meal planning, instead of fad diets, *Good Housekeeping* recommends that you follow the "three, four, five" rule: Breakfast should be no more than 300 calories, lunch no more than 400 calories, and dinner no more than 500 calories, plus two optional snacks of 100 to 200 calories apiece. These simple guidelines will help you gauge

how your consumption is measuring up day by day. (For more precise calorie recommendations based on gender, age, and activity level, visit healthierus.gov/dietaryguidelines.)

Lifetime weight maintenance requires setting reasonable weight goals for yourself and enjoying just enough of today's bounty to provide the energy you need for all you do. Make balance a habit; eat healthy food that pleases you and do exercises that you enjoy.

Focus on Flavor

While controlling the calories and total fats in the recipes you prepare is a primary concern, providing mealtime satisfaction is also essential to achieving and maintaining a healthy weight. A diet of low-cal, low-fat foods that aren't delicious and satisfying will soon be abandoned. If your family members are found foraging for their favorite snacks an hour after dinner (or make excuses to go out to dinner to avoid your cooking altogether), then you need to rethink your meal plans. The recipes you'll find in our *Light & Healthy Cooking* have been triple-tested and tasted in our kitchens with flavor and satiety in mind. We want you to discover how enjoyable healthy foods can be, so you and those you love will want to make them a long-term part of life.

We know there are many responsibilities competing for your time every day, so as we developed these light and healthy recipes to provide great taste and satisfaction, we never forgot that *quick and easy* is important when you have to get dinner on the table after a busy day. The recipes that made the cut require very

little hands-on time. They can either be prepared quickly and served, or mind themselves in the oven or on the stovetop while you do other things. Some can also be prepared ahead and simply reheated when the dinner hour strikes.

We believe a collection of easy and nutritious recipes that your family enjoys is worth a place in your kitchen, and we hope that the healthy eating patterns that they encourage will become a family tradition. You'll see: Light and healthy cooking is not only guilt-free—it can be habit forming.

The Nutrients You Need: The Big Three

Our bodies need three essential nutrients: carbohydrates, proteins, and fats.

CARBOHYDRATES: The right kind of carbohydrates is the mainstay of a well-balanced diet. "Good" carbohydrates include fruits, vegetables, beans, legumes, and whole grains. Carbohydrates can be made up of dietary fiber, starch or sugar, or a combo of the two. Those who follow a diet rich in dietary fiber have been shown to have a reduced risk of coronary heart disease, among other benefits, and research indicates that whole-grain eaters are thinner than people who eat few whole-grain foods. According to the latest USDA recommendations, at least half of your grains should be whole grains. Unfortunately, it is not always easy to tell if a product is a whole grain–rich food. For label-reading tips, see "How Do You Know It's Whole Grain?," opposite.

The starch and sugar in carbohydrates supply the body with the energy it needs for normal functions. When carbohydrates are digested, they become blood sugar (glucose),

HOW DO YOU KNOW IT'S WHOLE GRAIN?

Searching your supermarket for whole-grain foods can be confusing—so how do you separate the wheat from the chaff?

+ **LOOK FOR THE WORD *WHOLE* IN THE INGREDIENTS LIST.** Even though breads and crackers may be labeled *multigrain, nine-grain*, or *100 percent wheat bread*, that's no guarantee that any of them are whole grain. If an item is whole grain, the word *whole* will typically precede the grain's name in the ingredients panel: *whole-wheat flour* or *whole rye flour*, for example.

+ **NOTE WHERE THE WHOLE GRAIN FALLS IN THE LIST OF INGREDIENTS.** Ingredients are listed in order of their weight: If a whole grain is listed first and is the only grain, there is a lot of whole grain in the product. If the first ingredient is *wheat flour* (which is really white flour), followed by some sort of sweetener, then whole-wheat flour is not the dominant grain.

+ **BUY WHOLE GRAINS PACKAGED OR IN BULK.** The best way to ensure you are eating whole grains is to prepare them yourself. Throughout this book, we provide easy, satisfying recipes featuring a wide variety of whole grains, from barley and brown rice to wheat berries and oats. Give them a try!

+ **THE AMOUNT OF DIETARY FIBER WON'T HELP YOU IDENTIFY WHOLE GRAINS.** Different whole grains vary widely in fiber content: A full serving of whole grains—16 grams—will contain from just over a half gram of fiber to around 3 grams of fiber. And, in order to earn the label "High in Fiber" (5 grams of fiber or more), most foods contain added fiber (extra bran, resistant starch, or other fibers). For further information, visit wholegrainscouncil.org.

which is then used as fuel in our bodies. In general, the less added sugar you eat, the better. However, this doesn't include the naturally occurring sugar found in fruit, milk, or yogurt. The real culprit is the added sugar that comes from sweeteners, including white sugar, high-fructose corn syrup, brown rice syrup, dextrose, sucrose, fruit juice concentrate, and other sweeteners.

PROTEINS: The body needs protein to produce new body tissue. Proteins are also great for weight loss, as they help keep you feeling full for hours after eating. Too much protein, however, is unhealthy; it can stress the kidneys, and if it comes from fatty meat, it is also filling you with saturated fat. For optimum health, you should eat a variety of protein-containing foods, including seafood, lean meat and poultry, eggs, beans and lentils, soy products, and unsalted nuts and seeds. The latest USDA guidelines suggest that you eat more fish and nonmeat protein; try increasing the amount and variety that you consume by substituting seafood (or beans, lentils, tofu, or another soy product) in place of some of the meat and poultry you would typically eat. Whatever protein you prepare for dinner, ideally, your plate should look like this: half-filled with vegetables and/or fruits, a quarter with starches, and another quarter with protein-rich foods (and a little fat).

FATS: The USDA guideline for fat consumption is 20 to 35 percent of your total daily calories, which is a wide range. However, much more important than the total fat is the amount of saturated and trans fat in your diet. Here's what you need to know about these fats.

When an excess of saturated fat is consumed, it raises your blood cholesterol level, increasing your risk of heart disease and stroke. Saturated fat is found naturally in foods, but it is especially concentrated in fatty animal-based foods, such as fatty red meat, butter, and chicken skin, and in some oils, such as palm and coconut. Even "good" oils like olive and canola contain a little saturated fat, so you can't avoid it entirely. For a heart-healthy diet, you should derive less than 10 percent of your total calories from saturated fat, which is a maximum of 15 grams of saturated fat daily, based on a 1,500-calorie diet. Throughout the book, we have indicated heart-healthy recipes, containing 5 grams or less of saturated fat per serving, with the following icon: ♥. Our heart-healthy recipes also limit cholesterol and sodium; for specifics, see our guidelines on page 142.

Even worse than saturated fat is trans fat, which not only raises the LDL ("bad cholesterol") but also lowers the HDL ("good cholesterol"). It is formed by a process called hydrogenation, which turns oils into semisolids like margarine and shortening. The good news: The government is requiring manufacturers to list trans-fat amounts on labels, and many companies are removing the fat as a result. Still, trans fats are used in some packaged foods. On the ingredients list, these oils appear as *partially hydrogenated oils* or *shortening* and are reflected in the trans-fat total on the Nutrition Facts label. To keep your intake of trans fat low, use canola or olive oil whenever possible and "0 trans" or "trans-fat-free" spread. Eliminate processed foods made with partially hydrogenated oils, and limit those high in saturated fat.

Choose Your Plate

The USDA's My Plate icon is a simple visual representation of the foods that you should eat each day to achieve a healthy, balanced diet. It shows a dinner plate with quadrants for the four basic food groups: fruits and vegetables on one

half, grains and protein on the other plus a circle off to the side that denotes dairy. My Plate shows the relative importance of the different food groups. It replaces the USDA's Food Pyramid, which represented the food groups in colorful vertical bands with a staircase on the side that emphasized the importance of regular exercise in maintaining good health.

The My Plate icon is meant to serve as a reminder that helps you think about your food choices. It's paired with tips and suggestions, beginning with this commonsense advice that's right in line with GH's light and healthy eating guidelines: Enjoy your food, but eat less, avoiding oversized portions.

The My Plate plan advises on foods you should increase, so we've included lots of recipes in our *Light & Healthy Cooking* to support these efforts.

✦ **Make half your plate fruits and vegetables.** Vary your vegetables and don't forget fruits, whether they're fresh or frozen, canned (without added sweeteners) or dried.

✦ **Make at least half your grains whole grains.** Bread, pasta, oatmeal, breakfast cereals, and tortillas all provide opportunities to eat more whole grains.

✦ **Switch to fat-free (skim) or low-fat (1%) milk, yogurt, and cheese.** Note that calcium-fortified soy milk can meet your dairy requirements, too.

✦ **Go lean with protein.** Choose from lean cuts of meat and skinless poultry; fish and seafood; beans and peas; and soy products like tofu.

The plan also advises on foods to reduce. It notes that currently, many of the foods and beverages Americans eat and drink contain empty calories—solid fats and added sugars—that pack on the calories but deliver few or no nutrients. Limit the empty calories you consume from "junk food" like soda, candy, cakes, cookies, and pastries. Also limit foods high in saturated fat—like pizza and cheese—and especially those high in saturated fat and sodium—such as sausages, hot dogs, and bacon. Drink water instead of sugary drinks like sodas, sports drinks, and fruit drinks.

Because your food and physical activity choices each day affect your long-term health, the USDA has included interactive features on its website that help you customize and keep track of your diet and exercise: Visit myplate.gov to get started.

Interpreting Nutrition Information on Packages

While the Nutrition Facts label can tell you a lot about a food, you need to check the ingredients list to see what you're really eating. For example, is your breakfast cereal made with whole grains, or does your favorite salad dressing contain oil that is high in saturated fat?

UNDERSTANDING FOOD LABELS

Food labels help you make informed choices about the foods to include in your diet. The Percent Daily Values reflect the percentage of the recommended daily amount of a nutrient based on 2,000 calories daily. First, note the serving size. Sometimes even a small package holds multiple servings. Then budget your intake of nutrients by adding up calories and percentages. For example, this label shows that you get 27 percent of the daily value of saturated fat from one serving. If the next food you eat contains 25 percent of the recommended daily limit for saturated fat, then you have already consumed more than 50 per-cent of your total saturated fat allowance for that day.

When it comes to fat, saturated fat, sodium, and cholesterol, it's a good idea to keep the daily values under 100 percent. Fiber, vitamins A and C, calcium, and iron are listed, too, because diets often fall short; aim for 100 percent or more of these nutrients. (Other vitamins and minerals may also appear on food labels.)

The Daily Values footnote (not shown) includes a chart with some daily values for 2,000- and 2,500-calorie diets. Use these numbers as a guide. Your own daily values may be lower, depending on your calorie needs.

Nutrition Facts

Serving Size 2 pieces (29g)
Servings Per Container 15

Amount Per Serving

Calories 150	Calories from Fat 80

	% Daily Value*
Total Fat 8g	13%
Saturated Fat 5g	27%
Cholesterol 25mg	8%
Sodium 115mg	5%
Total Carbohydrate 18g	6%
Dietary Fiber 0g	0%
Sugars 6g	
Protein 2g	

Vitamin A 0%	•	Vitamin C 0%
Calcium 2%	•	Iron 2%

* Percent Daily Values are based on a 2,000 calorie diet.

By law, ingredients lists must be ordered by weight. The heaviest ingredient goes first, followed by the next-heaviest ingredient, and so on. It is not a good sign if sugar is among the first three ingredients listed in a cereal, or when bad fats like partially hydrogenated soybean and cottonseed oils are the third ingredient listed on a can of biscuit dough. Below is an explanation of common phrases found on many food packages:

"CHOLESTEROL FREE": Naturally cholesterol-free foods, by FDA regulations, can't be labeled "cholesterol free" unless they also say something like "Peanut butter, a cholesterol-free food," indicating that all peanut butters are, in fact, free of cholesterol. If you find this confusing just remember: Only foods of animal origin contain cholesterol. So, cookies made with butter or eggs will list cholesterol on the label, while crackers made with olive oil will not—unless they contain some other animal-derived product, like cheese.

"LIGHT": This word is used to describe fat content, taste, color, or consistency. If the manufacturer is describing the fat content as "light," the product has at least 50 percent less fat than the original. The label must also say "50% less fat than our regular product." "Light" olive oil, on the other hand, describes the oil's color. The oil is as caloric as regular olive oil but has been processed to remove some of its flavor. A muffin mix can say "light and fluffy" as a way to describe its texture or consistency.

"LOW-FAT" OR "FAT-FREE": Low-fat products must contain 3 grams or less fat per serving, and fat-free products must have less than 0.5 grams of fat per serving. But check the number of calories—that number could be very high. It is easy to gain lots of weight eating fat-free cookies because they are loaded with sugar.

"LOW SODIUM" OR "LIGHT IN SODIUM": This means that the sodium was cut by at least 50 percent compared to the original product. Be careful when using a "low-sodium" version of a super-high-sodium food such as soy sauce or soup. You can still end up consuming a lot of sodium. Check the numbers on the Nutrition Facts label.

"SUGAR-FREE," "NO ADDED SUGARS," "WITHOUT ADDED SUGARS": A sugar-free chocolate candy may not contain a speck of sugar, but it's still got plenty of fat and calories. Be sure to check out the Nutrition Facts label to know how many calories and grams of saturated fat you're consuming.

"SWEETENED WITH FRUIT JUICE," "FRUIT JUICE SWEETENER," OR "FRUIT JUICE CONCENTRATE": These sweeteners are made by reducing fruit juice—usually grape juice—into a sticky sweetener. These sweeteners are not nutritious; they are just like sugar.

Easy Changes You Can Make Right Now

Enjoying the benefits of a healthy lifestyle might require some changes, but they don't have to be painful. In fact, giving up your favorites forever should never be part of the program. There are actually a lot of small changes you can make that will be a big step in the right direction. Here are some of our favorites:

✦ **Go whole grain.** There are now more whole-grain choices than ever. In addition to the readily available bulk grains—from bulgur to millet to wheat berries—there's a multitude of whole-grain packaged foods available. Start with whole-wheat or multigrain pasta and whole-grain breads. Be sure to check bread labels to see how much of the rich brown color actually comes from whole grains rather than from coloring agents, cocoa, or molasses. (See "How Do You Know It's Whole Grain?," page 13, for more helpful pointers.)

✦ **Snack from the produce department.** Even if you are in a hurry, there are a lot of ready-to-eat fruit and vegetable choices in the produce department these days. If you don't see anything prepackaged that you want, go to the salad bar and select your own snack (then choose a reduced-fat or fat-free dressing and use it as a veggie dip).

✦ **Gradually switch to low-fat or fat-free milk and yogurt.** You'll be amazed how easy it is to downsize from whole to fat-free milk and yogurt if you do it in stages. Go to 2% for a few weeks, 1% for a while, and you are there. We'll bet you don't ever want to go back.

✦ **Explore reduced-fat, low-sodium options.** Many reduced-fat and low-sodium products will work well in your favorite family recipes. Grandma's lasagna might be just as delicious with reduced-fat cheeses and low-sodium toma-

LIGHT AND HEALTHY SHOPPING

Healthy lifestyle changes start in the supermarket; if you make the right selections there, your time in the kitchen will be easy. Here are some strategies for filling your cart and your cupboards with light, healthy, natural choices.

✦ Select a week's worth of recipes from our *Light & Healthy Cooking* and make a list of ingredients you will need for the planned meals.

✦ Discard high-fat items from your cupboards and add low-fat versions of your favorites to the list.

✦ Add one item from the snack aisle to the list so you won't feel deprived; make it the small size.

✦ Head for the market, but not until you have a healthy breakfast, lunch, or dinner. If you aren't hungry, you're not as likely to be tempted by unhealthy choices from the supermarket aisles.

✦ Check sell-by dates of groceries and select produce that is the freshest, even if it means adjusting your menu to make use of the best ingredients available.

✦ Compare Nutrition Facts labels among similar products and select those that best meet your dietary goals.

✦ Buy only what's on your list; don't be tempted by the end-of-aisle specials.

✦ Select the candy-free checkout lane; treat yourself to a magazine instead.

toes. In fact, if they had been in her local market, she probably would have used them to produce healthy meals for her family.

✦ **Always read the Nutrition Facts labels.** It doesn't take a lot of time and you can learn a lot. Sometimes those packages with the biggest fat-free, low-fat, or low-salt labels are very high in sugar and calories. (See "Understanding Food Labels," page 16).

✦ **Break high-calorie combos.** Discover bread with a little hummus (instead of butter), baked potatoes with herbs (try nonfat Greek yogurt instead of sour cream), dessert without whipped cream (or ice cream)—you'll enjoy the food's flavor even more.

✦ **Take control of salt.** The latest USDA guidelines recommend reducing your daily sodium intake to less than 2,300 milligrams; they recommend further reducing it to 1,500 milligrams for people who are 51 and older and those of any age who have hypertension, diabetes, or chronic kidney disease. That's a tall order, especially if you like to cook with prepared sauces and seasoning packets and spice mixtures. These products are convenient, to be sure, but watch out for the hidden salt. Look for reduced-sodium versions and add only as much as you need.

✦ **Remember, liquid calories count.** The number of calories in beverages might shock you. Fruit juice, alcoholic drinks, sweetened lemonade and iced tea, soda, and especially lattés and other gourmet coffee drinks are loaded with empty calories. And, on a warm day, you might go ahead and have a refill.

✦ **Walk to your local ice cream store**—or drive if it is really too far to walk. Just don't keep that half-gallon in the freezer. You don't need to deny yourself your favorite treat, but if enjoying a bowl of ice cream requires a trip, you have to think about it—and it becomes a special occasion. Or dip into some frozen yogurt or sorbet for a lower-calorie treat.

Light and Healthy Cooking Techniques

Often, great flavor comes as much from how a food is prepared as from the food itself. We use the following high-flavor, low-fat cooking techniques in recipes throughout the book. Some are slow, others fast, but all can be low maintenance. Make them a part of your light and healthy cooking repertoire.

BRAISING AND STEWING: Few dishes satisfy as much as a long-simmered stew or braised pot roast. Braising is usually done in a Dutch oven or heavy-bottomed pot with a tight-fitting lid and a handle at each side. For the richest flavor, brown the meat or poultry (first cut into chunks if you're making stew), add vegetables and a small amount of stock or water, cover tightly, and simmer. Patience is key: Even the toughest cuts of meat will become meltingly tender through this moist-heat method, but it takes a long time for the collagen in meat to break down. Tip: Do not let the liquid cook at more than a slow simmer or the meat will end up dry and tough.

ROASTING: Slow-cooking meat, poultry, whole fish, vegetables, and even fruits in the oven intensifies their natural flavors. The interior of the food becomes succulent and tender, while the exterior develops a delightfully caramelized crust. You'll need a heavy, shallow roasting pan; place it, uncovered, on a rack in the center of the oven so the hot air can circulate freely. When you're roasting vegetables or fruit, spread them out in a single layer or they will steam instead of caramelizing. Tip: The only way to guarantee that meat or poultry is roasted to the desired doneness is a meat thermometer. To ensure an accurate reading, always insert the thermometer into the center or thickest part of the roast without touching any bone or fatty sections.

BAKING: Meat, poultry, and seafood can be baked in covered cookware with a little liquid, which ensures that items like chicken breasts and fish won't dry out during cooking. Or fill packets made from aluminum foil or parchment paper with the ingredients (potatoes or other root vegetables work nicely) and seal tightly; the packets keep moisture and flavor in—and

require a minimum of cleanup. Tip: Before sealing the packets, toss in some lemon slices or sprigs of fresh herbs, such as rosemary or thyme, for added flavor.

GRILLING: Whether you grill outdoors on a gas or charcoal grill or indoors in a ridged grill pan, the intense heat caramelizes the crust and lends delicious smoky flavor to whatever meat, poultry, seafood, or vegetable you're grilling. Much of the fat drips away during the process, making this quick and easy method an excellent choice for those looking to lighten up. Tip: To intensify flavor, use a dry rub or marinade. Use the leftover marinade to baste the food as it cooks.

STIR-FRYING: The fastest of cooking methods, stir-frying yields quick, tasty results and requires only a small amount of oil. Small pieces of food are cooked over high heat in a wok or skillet, stirred constantly to keep the food from sticking or burning. Vegetables should be sliced or chopped to roughly the same size to ensure even cooking; the fastest-cooking ingredients should be the last items you add to the pan. Lean cuts of meat should be sliced very thinly across the grain or cubed. Shrimp can be stir-fried with their shells on or off. Tip: When a recipe calls for soy sauce, use the reduced-sodium kind or dilute regular soy sauce with water.

STEAMING: Cooking vegetables in a steamer basket over simmering water is a smart choice for light and healthy cooking. Steaming preserves the veggies' natural color, flavor, and nutritional value, and it doesn't require any added fat. Tip: You can also steam vegetables in the microwave. For instructions and cook times for individual vegetables, see "Easy Microwave-Steamed Vegetables," page 130.

ABOUT THE RECIPES

We've selected the recipes in this book according to our light and healthy guidelines. With a few exceptions, they are low calorie. At *Good Housekeeping*, that means a maximum of 450 calories per serving for main dishes that include a starch or fruit and 300 calories for main dishes without. All other courses should be 150 calories or less. The handful of breakfast, side, and dessert recipes that contain more than 150 calories per serving can easily be incorporated into meals or snacks that meet our "three, four, five" calories guidelines; see page 11.

Since eating less saturated fat should be on the agenda for all of us, we've included heart-healthy recipes that not only limit saturated fat, but also limit cholesterol and sodium. (For a breakdown, see Index of Recipes by Icon, page 142). And, because fiber provides a host of health benefits, from promoting good digestion and weight loss to quelling hunger, we've also called out main and side dishes that are high in fiber (contain 5 grams of fiber or more per serving).

If keeping track of this nutritional information seems labor-intensive, don't worry: We do the work for you. At the end of every recipe, you'll find complete nutritional information that lists the approximate calories (and percentage of calories from fat), protein, carbohydrates, total and saturated fat, fiber, cholesterol, and sodium content per serving. The nutritional information is followed by the colorful icons shown above to help you quickly identify recipes by your category of choice, from 30-minute or make-ahead meals to heart-healthy and high-fiber options.

Our nutritional calculations do not include any optional ingredients or garnishes, and when alternative ingredients are listed (such as margarine instead of butter), our calculations are based on the first item listed. Unless we note low-fat or reduced-fat dairy products, whole-fat milk, yogurt, and cheese has been used. But we invite you to swap in reduced-fat or nonfat products to create even lighter meals. If you're keeping tabs on your sodium intake, you should also feel free to substitute low-sodium broths, no-salt-added beans, and reduced-sodium soy sauce. In fact, we could all make this a habit!

1

Breakfast

You've heard it before but we'll say it again: A good breakfast is the foundation of any healthy diet. And because nothing kick-starts your day like a serving of fill-you-up fiber, we've provided an assortment of high-fiber offerings. If mornings are hectic at your house, try our multigrain cereal—it takes just five minutes to prepare. Or bake our reduced-fat granola ahead of time and, come morning, layer it with berries and vanilla yogurt for a sweet and satsifying parfait. For more on the benefits of fiber, see "Fiber: The Fabulous Fat Fighter" (page 25).

If you want to take breakfast on the go, bake up a batch of our banana bread. Grab a slice and a piece of fruit and you have a healthy breakfast you can pack in your purse. We offer two equally tempting options for those of you who like preparing breakfast in a blender: One includes strawberries, mango or apricot nectar, and yogurt, the other gives bananas, peanut butter, and soy milk a whirl.

We also provide light and healthy options just right for leisurely mornings or weekend brunches, including an assortment of egg dishes. Eggs are a high-quality source of protein—especially the egg white. Thus, our omelet and soufflé recipes are made with a combination of eggs and egg whites—and loaded with veggies—so you can eat them without guilt. And, because everyone needs a little sweetness in their life, we've shared healthier whole-grain takes on favorites like pancakes.

Granola-Yogurt Parfaits (recipe page 26)

Mango-Strawberry Smoothie

A healthy and colorful morning lift off! Either way you make it—with mango or with apricot nectar—this is a wonderful combination. If you use frozen strawberries, skip the ice cubes.

TOTAL TIME: 5 minutes

MAKES: 2½ cups or 2 servings

1   cup fresh or frozen unsweetened strawberries

1   cup mango or apricot nectar, chilled

½   cup plain or vanilla yogurt

4   ice cubes

In blender, combine strawberries, mango nectar, yogurt, and ice and blend until mixture is smooth and frothy. Pour into 2 tall glasses. Serve with straws, if you like.

EACH SERVING: About 125 calories (7 percent calories from fat), 4g protein, 27g carbohydrate, 1g total fat (0g saturated), 0g fiber, 3mg cholesterol, 44mg sodium ♥ ♥

EAT YOUR STRAWBERRIES

These days, strawberries are easy to find all year long, but they are at their sweet, juicy peak in spring. Delicious and nutritious, twelve medium berries weigh in at 45 calories, 3 grams fiber, and about 135 percent of the daily recommended requirement for vitamin C.

Banana-Peanut Butter Smoothie

For a thicker, colder smoothie, cut peeled banana into chunks and freeze up to one week in a self-sealing plastic bag.

TOTAL TIME: 5 minutes

MAKES: 1½ cups or 1 serving

1   small ripe banana, cut in half

½   cup soy milk

1   teaspoon creamy natural peanut butter

3   ice cubes

In blender, combine banana, soy milk, peanut butter, and ice cubes; blend until mixture is smooth and frothy.

EACH SERVING: About 165 calories (22 percent calories from fat), 6g protein, 28g carbohydrate, 4g total fat (2g saturated), 2g fiber, 5mg cholesterol, 85mg sodium ♥

Five-Minute Multigrain Cereal

Get a great-grains start to your day with a hot and tasty serving of three kinds of grains in five minutes. For photo, see page 11.

TOTAL TIME: 5 minutes

MAKES: 1 serving

2   tablespoons quick-cooking barley

2   tablespoons bulgur

2   tablespoons old-fashioned oats, uncooked

2/3 cup water

2   tablespoons raisins

pinch ground cinnamon

1   tablespoon chopped walnuts or pecans

low-fat milk or soy milk (optional)

In microwave-safe 1-quart bowl, combine barley, bulgur, oats, and water. Microwave on High 2 minutes. Stir in raisins and cinnamon; microwave 3 minutes longer. Stir, then top with walnuts and, if you like, milk.

EACH SERVING: About 265 calories (20 percent calories from fat), 8g protein, 50g carbohydrate, 6g total fat (1g saturated), 7g fiber, 0mg cholesterol, 5mg sodium ●

FIBER: THE FABULOUS FAT FIGHTER

Switching to a high-fiber diet can be like taking a magic weight-loss pill. But how exactly does fiber work?

✦ IT'S FILLING. It swells a little in the stomach, quelling hunger. So, a 100-calorie portion of Kellogg's All Bran (18 grams fiber) will make you feel a lot fuller than a 100-calorie portion of Kellogg's Corn Flakes (1 gram fiber).

✦ IT LOWERS BLOOD SUGAR. Many high-fiber foods (think oatmeal) help moderate your blood sugar level and keep your insulin level normal. Lower insulin has been linked to lower body fat and a lower risk of diabetes.

✦ IT FLUSHES OUT FAT. Some types of fiber, particularly those in fruits and vegetables, can sweep out fat before the body absorbs it.

✦ IT'S LOW CAL. Pure fiber itself has virtually no calories. Your body can't break it down, so it runs right through your digestive system, providing only bulk. That's why high-fiber foods are usually lower in calories than low-fiber foods. For example, a cup of apple juice has no fiber and 117 calories; a cup of sliced, unpeeled apple has 34 grams fiber and 74 calories.

GOOD SOURCES OF FIBER: Fruits, vegetables, legumes, brans, breads, cereals, pasta, and starchy foods made with whole grains. (See "How Do You Know It's Whole Grain?," page 13, and "Get Your Grains" boxes throughout the book.)

Lower-Fat Granola

We baked oats, almonds, quinoa, wheat germ, and sesame seeds with apple juice instead of oil.

ACTIVE TIME: 10 minutes
TOTAL TIME: 45 minutes
MAKES: 6 cups or 12 servings

4   cups old-fashioned oats, uncooked
½   cup honey
½   cup apple juice
1½   teaspoons vanilla extract
¾   teaspoon ground cinnamon
½   cup natural almonds
½   cup quinoa, thoroughly rinsed
¼   cup toasted wheat germ
2   tablespoons sesame seeds
½   cup dried apricots, cut into ¼-inch dice
½   cup dark seedless raisins

1. Preheat oven to 350°F. Place oats in two 15½" by 10½" jelly-roll pans. Bake until lightly toasted, about 15 minutes, stirring twice.

2. In large bowl, with wire whisk, mix honey, apple juice, vanilla, and cinnamon until blended. Add toasted oats, almonds, quinoa, wheat germ, and sesame seeds; stir well to coat.

3. Spread oat mixture evenly in same jelly-roll pans; bake until golden brown, 20 to 25 minutes, stirring frequently. Cool in pans on wire rack.

4. When cool, transfer granola to large bowl; stir in apricots and raisins. Store at room temperature in air-tight container up to 1 month.

EACH ½-CUP SERVING: About 350 calories (21 percent calories from fat), 12g protein, 64g carbohydrate, 8g total fat (2g saturated), 8g fiber, 0mg cholesterol, 10mg sodium 🍽

Granola-Yogurt Parfait

A healthy breakfast doesn't get any easier than this. For photo, see page 22.

TOTAL TIME: 5 minutes
MAKES: 1 serving

½   cup fresh or frozen (partially thawed) raspberries or other favorite berry
¾   cup vanilla low-fat yogurt
2   tablespoons Lower-Fat Granola (left)

Into parfait glass or wineglass, spoon some of the raspberries, vanilla yogurt, and granola. Repeat layering until all ingredients are used.

EACH SERVING: About 255 calories (11 percent calories from fat), 10g protein, 47g carbohydrate, 3g total fat (2g saturated), 5g fiber, 12mg cholesterol, 160mg sodium ⊘

EAT YOUR YOGURT

Need to fit more calcium and protein into your diet? This creamy, tangy snack is the way to go. Any low-fat or nonfat all-natural brand has health benefits (it contains bacteria that aids in digestion, for starters), but we really love Greek-style yogurt. This special, strained yogurt has a dense texture and rich flavor—even the nonfat versions. Perk up plain yogurt with add-ins like fresh fruit, honey, reduced-fat granola, and nuts. Or, swap mayo or sour cream for yogurt to create low-fat dips and dressings. Greek yogurt is so creamy, it can even be used in some sauces to replace butter or cream.

Garden Vegetable Omelet

This is a mostly egg-white omelet with two whole eggs (and even a little feta) added for richness. Fill 'er up with red potatoes, onion, pepper, zucchini and fresh basil, and you have a healthy and flavorful start to your day.

ACTIVE TIME: 30 minutes
TOTAL TIME: 45 minutes

MAKES: 4 servings

8	ounces red potatoes, cut into ½-inch pieces
1	onion, finely chopped
1	red pepper, cut into ½-inch pieces
1	green pepper, cut into ½-inch pieces
1	small zucchini (8 ounces), cut into ½-inch pieces
¾	teaspoon salt
¼	teaspoon coarsely ground black pepper
¼	cup water
4	tablespoons chopped fresh basil leaves
6	large egg whites
2	large eggs
½	cup crumbled feta cheese (2 ounces)

1. In small saucepan, heat potatoes and enough *water* to cover to boiling over high heat. Reduce heat to low; cover and simmer until tender, about 10 minutes. Drain.

2. Spray 12-inch nonstick skillet with cooking spray. Add onion and cook over medium heat until golden, about 5 minutes. Add red and green peppers, zucchini, salt, and black pepper and cook, stirring frequently, until vegetables are tender-crisp. Stir in water and heat to boiling. Reduce to low; cover and simmer until vegetables are tender, 10 minutes. Remove skillet from heat; stir in potatoes and 1 tablespoon basil.

3. Preheat oven to 375°F. In medium bowl, with wire whisk or fork, mix egg whites, eggs, ¼ cup feta, and remaining 3 tablespoons basil.

4. Spray oven-safe 10-inch skillet with non-stick cooking spray. Pour egg mixture into pan and cook over medium-high heat until egg mixture begins to set, 1 to 2 minutes. Remove skillet from heat. With slotted spoon, spread vegetable mixture over egg mixture in skillet; sprinkle with remaining ¼ cup feta. Bake until omelet sets, 10 minutes. If you like, broil 1 to 2 minutes to brown top of omelet.

EACH SERVING: About 185 calories (29 percent calories from fat), 13g protein, 20g carbohydrate, 6g total fat (3g saturated), 3g fiber, 119mg cholesterol, 860mg sodium

Spinach Soufflé

Even though this recipe requires about 40 minutes total, only 20 minutes is active prep. During the remaining time, while the soufflé bakes, you can relax!

ACTIVE TIME: 20 minutes
TOTAL TIME: 40 minutes
MAKES: 4 main-dish servings

3	tablespoons plain dried bread crumbs

nonstick cooking spray

1½	cups low-fat (1%) milk
⅓	cup cornstarch
2	large eggs, separated
1	package (10 ounces) frozen chopped spinach, thawed and squeezed dry
3	tablespoons grated Parmesan cheese
½	teaspoon salt
¼	teaspoon coarsely ground black pepper
½	teaspoon cream of tartar
4	large egg whites

1. Preheat oven to 425°F. Spray 10-inch quiche dish or shallow 2-quart casserole with cooking spray and sprinkle with bread crumbs to coat. Set aside.

2. In 2-quart saucepan, with wire whisk, beat milk with cornstarch until blended. Heat milk mixture over medium-high heat until mixture thickens and boils, stirring constantly. Boil 1 minute. Remove saucepan from heat.

3. In large bowl, with rubber spatula, mix egg yolks, spinach, Parmesan, salt, and pepper until blended; stir in warm milk mixture. Cool slightly (if spinach mixture is too warm, it will deflate beaten egg whites when folded in).

4. In another large bowl, with mixer at high speed, beat cream of tartar and egg whites until stiff peaks form. Gently fold egg-white mixture, one-third at a time, into spinach mixture.

5. Spoon soufflé mixture into quiche dish. Bake 20 minutes or until top is golden and puffed. Serve immediately.

EACH SERVING: About 195 calories (23 percent calories from fat), 15g protein, 23g carbohydrate, 5g total fat (2g saturated), 2g fiber, 114mg cholesterol, 590mg sodium

Whole-Grain Pancakes

Have a stack of pancakes without a side of guilt. These flapjacks contain healthy oats and whole-wheat flour. Plus they're topped with delicious fresh fruit.

ACTIVE TIME: 15 minutes
TOTAL TIME: 30 minutes

MAKES: 12 pancakes or 4 main-dish servings

2   ripe peaches, pitted and chopped
½   pint raspberries (1½ cups)
1   tablespoon sugar
½   cup all-purpose flour
½   cup whole-wheat flour
½   cup quick-cooking oats, uncooked
2   teaspoons baking powder
½   teaspoon salt
1¼   cups skim milk
1   large egg, lightly beaten
1   tablespoon vegetable oil

1. In medium bowl, combine peaches, raspberries, and sugar. Stir to coat; set aside.

2. Meanwhile, in large bowl, combine flours, oats, baking powder, and salt. Add milk, egg, and oil; stir just until flour mixture is moistened; batter will be lumpy.

3. Spray 12-inch nonstick skillet with cooking spray; heat on medium 1 minute. Pour batter by scant ¼ cups into skillet, making about 4 pancakes at a time. Cook until tops are bubbly, some bubbles burst, and edges look dry. With wide spatula, turn pancakes and cook until undersides are golden. Transfer pancakes to platter. Cover; keep warm.

4. Repeat with remaining batter, using more nonstick cooking spray if necessary.

5. To serve, top with fruit mixture.

EACH SERVING: About 275 calories (20 percent calories from fat), 10g protein, 46g carbohydrate, 6g total fat (1g saturated), 6g fiber, 55mg cholesterol, 545mg sodium ♥ ⊛

Spiced Apple Pancake

This simple pancake makes delightful brunch fare. For the puffiest pancake, use a cast-iron skillet. If you don't have one, choose a heavy 12-inch skillet with a bottom that is at least 10 inches in diameter and an oven-safe handle.

ACTIVE TIME: 5 minutes
TOTAL TIME: 35 minutes

MAKES: 8 main-dish servings

2	tablespoons butter or margarine
2	tablespoons water
½	cup plus 2 tablespoons sugar
1½	pounds Granny Smith apples (3 to 4 medium), peeled, cored, and cut into 8 wedges
3	large eggs
¾	cup milk
¾	cup all-purpose flour
1	teaspoon pumpkin pie spice or ½ teaspoon ground cinnamon
¼	teaspoon salt

1. Preheat oven to 450°F. In 12-inch cast-iron skillet, heat butter, water, and ½ cup sugar over medium-high heat to boiling. Add apple wedges; cook 12 to 15 minutes or until apples are golden and sugar mixture begins to caramelize, stirring occasionally.

2. Meanwhile, in blender or food processor with knife blade attached, place eggs and milk. Add flour, pumpkin pie spice, salt, and remaining 2 tablespoons sugar. Blend until batter is smooth.

3. When apple mixture in skillet is deep golden, pour batter over apples. Place skillet in oven; bake 15 to 17 minutes or until puffed and lightly browned. Serve immediately.

EACH SERVING: About 210 calories (26 percent calories from fat), 5g protein, 36g carbohydrate, 6g total fat (3g saturated), 2g fiber, 91mg cholesterol, 140mg sodium ♥

Low-Fat Banana Bread

We used egg whites and unsweetened applesauce to slim down everyone's favorite quick bread without sacrificing moisture. For a whole-grain variation, substitute ½ cup whole-wheat flour for the same amount of all-purpose flour.

ACTIVE TIME: 20 minutes
TOTAL TIME: 1 hour
MAKES: 1 loaf, 16 slices

1¾ cups all-purpose flour

½ cup sugar

1 teaspoon baking powder

½ teaspoon baking soda

½ teaspoon salt

1 cup mashed very ripe bananas (2 medium)

⅓ cup unsweetened applesauce

2 large egg whites

1 large egg

¼ cup pecans, chopped

1. Preheat oven to 350°F. Grease 9" by 5" metal loaf pan. In large bowl, combine flour, sugar, baking powder, baking soda, and salt. In medium bowl, with fork, mix bananas, applesauce, egg whites, and egg until well blended. Stir banana mixture into flour mixture just until flour mixture is moistened.

GO NUTS!

Dieters have long viewed nuts as the enemy. Sure, they're high in fat and calories—but eaten in moderation (2 tablespoons daily), nuts can do wonders. By adding a bit of fat to a fat-free meal like cereal and skim milk, nuts can slow down the emptying of your stomach, making you feel fuller longer. In addition, nuts may suppress the appetite longer than other fatty foods do. Buy nuts roasted and unsalted for big flavor without the sodium. Or spread a little peanut butter—or almond or cashew butter—on your morning toast.

2. Pour batter into prepared pan; sprinkle with chopped pecans. Bake until toothpick inserted in center comes out almost clean, 40 to 45 minutes. Cool in pan on wire rack 10 minutes; remove from pan and cool completely on wire rack.

EACH SERVING: About 120 calories (15 percent calories from fat), 3g protein, 23g carbohydrate, 2g total fat (0g saturated), 1g fiber, 13mg cholesterol, 155mg sodium ♥ ▬

2

Salads, Soups & Sandwiches

Salad, in its most familiar guise, is composed of cool, crisp greens tossed with a piquant dressing. But a winning salad can be created from an endless array of ingredients and bolstered with chicken, meat, or seafood to create a meal in a bowl. High-fat dressings are often the downfall of otherwise healthy salads, so we offer five recipes for skinny salad dressings that contain 15 calories or less and zero grams of fat per serving.

Whether you favor a stockpot or a slow cooker, soups are one-pot cooking at its finest. Here you'll find wholesome recipes that'll ensure you're filling that pot with fiber-rich grains and beans, vitamin-packed veggies, and lean poultry and meat. We have cool, refreshing soups that require little to no cooking, like chilled buttermilk and corn soup, as well as traditional warm, soothing soups and hearty chili and beef stew. We also provide recipes for homemade veggie and chicken broths, which are healthier and tastier than the high-sodium canned varieties.

Sandwiches are not off-limits in a light and healthy meal plan. You just have to choose your bread *and* your fillings with care, and we offer satisfying low-cal options you can sink your teeth into without guilt. You'll find tasty options for a quick, healthy lunch, like roast beef sandwiches. On hectic weeknights or lazy weekends, our turkey fajitas or chicken quesadillas will keep everybody happy. Or, if your family is clamoring to grill, serve up one of our chicken-burger variations or our mini barbecue pork sandwiches.

Curried Chicken Salad with Cantaloupe Slaw (recipe page 36)

Skinny Salad Dressings

These flavor-packed drizzles are so good, you'll forget you're eating low fat.

Honey-Lime Vinaigrette

TOTAL TIME: 5 minutes

MAKES: 1/2 cup or 8 servings

1/3 cup fresh lime juice (from 2 to 3 limes)
4 teaspoons honey
1 tablespoon rice vinegar
1/8 teaspoon salt

In small bowl, with wire whisk, mix lime juice, honey, vinegar, and salt until blended. Cover and refrigerate up to 3 days.

EACH TABLESPOON: About 15 calories (0 percent calories from fat), 0g protein, 4g carbohydrate, 0g total fat, 0g fiber, 0mg cholesterol, 37mg sodium 💚 🖤

Tomato-Orange Vinaigrette

TOTAL TIME: 5 minutes

MAKES: 1/2 cup or 8 servings

1/2 cup tomato juice
1 tablespoon balsamic vinegar
1/4 teaspoon grated orange peel
1/4 teaspoon sugar
1/4 teaspoon ground black pepper

In small bowl, with wire whisk, mix tomato juice, vinegar, orange peel, sugar, and pepper until blended. Cover and refrigerate up to 3 days.

EACH TABLESPOON: About 5 calories (0 percent calories from fat), 0g protein, 1g carbohydrate, 0g total fat, 0g fiber, 0mg cholesterol, 55mg sodium 💚 🖤

Orange-Ginger Dressing

TOTAL TIME: 5 minutes

MAKES: 1 cup or 16 servings

1/2 cup seasoned rice vinegar
1/2 cup orange juice
1/2 teaspoon grated, peeled fresh ginger
1/2 teaspoon soy sauce
1/8 teaspoon Asian sesame oil

In small bowl, with wire whisk, mix vinegar, orange juice, ginger, soy sauce, and sesame oil until blended. Cover and refrigerate up to 5 days.

EACH TABLESPOON: About 10 calories (0 percent calories from fat), 0g protein, 3g carbohydrate, 0g total fat, 0g fiber, 0mg cholesterol, 110mg sodium 💚 🖤

Buttermilk-Chive Dressing

TOTAL TIME: 5 minutes

MAKES: 3/4 cup or 12 servings

1/2 cup reduced-fat buttermilk
2 tablespoons distilled white vinegar
2 tablespoons chopped fresh chives
1 tablespoon low-fat mayonnaise
1/4 teaspoon salt
1/4 teaspoon ground black pepper

In small bowl, with wire whisk, mix buttermilk, vinegar, chives, dressing, salt, and pepper until blended. Cover and refrigerate up to 3 days.

EACH TABLESPOON: About 6 calories (0 percent calories from fat), 0g protein, 1g carbohydrate, 0g total fat, 0g fiber, 0mg cholesterol, 65mg sodium 💚 🖤

Creamy Ranch Dressing

TOTAL TIME: 5 minutes

MAKES: 1 cup or 16 servings

¾ cup plain nonfat yogurt

¼ cup low-fat mayonnaise

1 green onion, minced

1 tablespoon cider vinegar

2 teaspoons Dijon mustard

¼ teaspoon dried thyme

¼ teaspoon coarsely ground black pepper

In small bowl, with wire whisk, mix yogurt, mayonnaise, green onion, vinegar, mustard, thyme, and pepper until blended. Cover and refrigerate up to 5 days.

EACH TABLESPOON: About 15 calories (0 percent calories from fat), 1g protein, 2g carbohydrate, 0g total fat, 0g fiber, 0mg cholesterol, 60mg sodium ♥ ♥

GIVE IT A LIFT WITH CITRUS

Grated peel or a splash of juice can perk up almost anything sweet or savory—without adding fat. Just a sprinkle or squeeze before serving can make the difference between a plain dish and a memorable one. Try these simple, flavor-boosting ideas.

GRATED PEEL

✦ Stir any citrus peel into rice pilaf to transform it from simple to sumptuous.

✦ Toss orange peel with lightly buttered carrots or roasted sweet potatoes.

✦ Sprinkle lime peel over coconut sorbet for a zesty fresh flavor.

JUICE

✦ Squirt some lemon, lime, or orange juice over steamed shellfish or grilled chicken just before eating.

✦ Add some lemon juice to bottled low-fat salad dressing to give it a sprightly homemade taste.

✦ Stir some lime juice into canned black bean or lentil soup to add zip before serving.

GRATED PEEL AND JUICE

✦ Stir grated lemon peel and juice into a tablespoon of low-fat mayonnaise for a tangy sandwich spread or dressing for steamed asparagus.

✦ Grate any citrus peel into a bowl with a tablespoon of butter or margarine, and add a squirt of juice plus a pinch of dried herb to make a citrus butter. Toss with cooked vegetables.

✦ Combine grated lime peel and juice with minced fresh ginger. Stir into a fruit salad (bananas, cantaloupe, and blueberries would be a nice match).

Curried Chicken Salad with Cantaloupe Slaw

Here, curry, crystallized ginger, and crushed red pepper bring out the full sweet flavor of fresh fruit. For photo, see page 32.

ACTIVE TIME: 25 minutes
TOTAL TIME: 35 minutes plus marinating
MAKES: 4 main-dish servings

1 to 2 limes
1   container (6 ounces) plain low-fat yogurt
¾   teaspoon curry powder
¼   cup chopped crystallized ginger
1   teaspoon salt
¼   teaspoon crushed red pepper
4   medium skinless, boneless chicken breast halves (about 1¼ pounds)
½   small cantaloupe, rind removed, cut into julienne strips (2 cups)
1   large mango, peeled and cut into julienne strips (2 cups)
½   cup loosely packed fresh cilantro leaves, chopped
1   head Boston lettuce
lime wedges (optional)

1. Prepare outdoor grill for covered direct grilling over medium heat.

2. From limes, grate ½ teaspoon peel and squeeze 2 tablespoons juice. In large bowl, with wire whisk, combine 1 tablespoon lime juice and ¼ teaspoon lime peel with yogurt, curry powder, 2 tablespoons ginger, ¾ teaspoon salt, and ⅛ teaspoon crushed red pepper. Add chicken, turning to coat with marinade. Cover and let stand 15 minutes at room temperature or 30 minutes in refrigerator, turning occasionally.

3. Meanwhile, prepare slaw: In medium bowl, with rubber spatula, gently stir cantaloupe and mango with cilantro, remaining 2 tablespoons ginger, 1 tablespoon lime juice, ¼ teaspoon lime peel, ¼ teaspoon salt, and ⅛ teaspoon crushed red pepper; set aside. Makes about 4 cups.

4. Grease grill rack. Remove chicken from marinade; discard marinade. Place chicken on hot rack. Cover grill and cook chicken 10 to 12 minutes or until juices run clear when thickest part of breast is pierced with tip of knife, turning chicken over once. Transfer chicken to cutting board; cool slightly until easy to handle, then cut into long thin slices.

5. To serve, arrange lettuce leaves on four dinner plates; top with chicken and slaw. Serve with lime wedges, if you like.

EACH SERVING CHICKEN WITH LETTUCE: About 205 calories (18 percent calories from fat), 34g protein, 5g carbohydrate, 4g total fat (1g saturated), 1g fiber, 92mg cholesterol, 330mg sodium ♥

EACH ½ CUP SLAW: About 50 calories (0 percent calories from fat), 1g protein, 13g carbohydrate, 0g total fat, 1g fiber, 0mg cholesterol, 150mg sodium ♥

Black-Bean and Avocado Salad

A satisfying combination of summer veggies, romaine lettuce, and black beans tossed with a creamy buttermilk dressing. This salad would also be good with our Creamy Ranch Dressing or Honey-Lime Vinaigrette (pages 34–35).

TOTAL TIME: 20 minutes

MAKES: 4 main-dish servings

Buttermilk-Chive Dressing (page 34)

1 small head romaine lettuce (about 1 pound), cut into ¾-inch pieces (about 8 cups)

2 medium tomatoes, cut into ½-inch pieces

2 Kirby cucumbers (about 4 ounces each), unpeeled, each cut lengthwise into quarters, then crosswise into ¼-inch-thick pieces

1 ripe avocado, cut into ½-inch pieces

1 can (15 to 19 ounces) black beans, rinsed and drained

1. Prepare Buttermilk-Chive Dressing.

2. In large serving bowl, combine romaine, tomatoes, cucumbers, avocado, and beans. Add dressing and toss until evenly coated.

EACH SERVING: About 235 calories (23 percent calories from fat), 11g protein, 36g carbohydrate, 6g fat (1g saturated), 15g fiber, 0mg cholesterol, 521mg sodium ● ⓥ

Tex-Mex Turkey Cobb Salad

Warm Southwestern accents give this classic a new attitude.

TOTAL TIME: 30 minutes

MAKES: 4 main-dish servings

¼ cup fresh lime juice

2 tablespoons chopped fresh cilantro leaves

4 teaspoons olive oil

1 teaspoon sugar

¼ teaspoon ground cumin

¼ teaspoon salt

¼ teaspoon coarsely ground black pepper

1 medium head romaine lettuce (1¼ pounds), trimmed and leaves cut into ½-inch-wide strips

1 pint cherry tomatoes, each cut into quarters

12 ounces cooked skinless roast turkey meat, cut into ½-inch pieces (2 cups)

1 can (15 to 19 ounces) pinto beans, rinsed and drained

2 small cucumbers (6 ounces each), peeled, seeded, and sliced ½ inch thick

1. Prepare dressing: In small bowl, with wire whisk, combine lime juice, cilantro, oil, sugar, cumin, salt, and pepper.

2. Place lettuce in large serving bowl. Arrange tomatoes, turkey, beans, and cucumbers in rows over lettuce and present the salad. Just before serving, toss salad with dressing.

EACH SERVING: About 310 calories (20 percent calories from fat), 39g protein, 32g carbohydrate, 7g total fat (1g saturated), 13g fiber, 71mg cholesterol, 505mg sodium ● ⓥ

Tomato and Mint Tabbouleh

Tabbouleh, the popular bulgur wheat and vegetable salad, is one of the best ways to enjoy tomatoes, cucumbers, and herbs.

TOTAL TIME: 20 minutes plus standing and chilling

MAKES: 12 side-dish servings

1½	cups boiling water
1½	cups bulgur
¼	cup fresh lemon juice
1	pound ripe tomatoes (3 medium), cut into ½-inch pieces
1	medium cucumber (8 ounces), peeled and cut into ½-inch pieces
3	green onions, chopped
¾	cup loosely packed fresh flat-leaf parsley leaves, chopped
½	cup loosely packed fresh mint leaves, chopped
1	tablespoon olive oil
¾	teaspoon salt
¼	teaspoon coarsely ground black pepper

1. In medium bowl, combine water, bulgur, and lemon juice, stirring to mix. Let stand until liquid has been absorbed, about 30 minutes.

2. To bulgur mixture, add tomatoes, cucumber, green onions, parsley, mint, oil, salt, and pepper, stirring to mix. Cover and refrigerate to blend flavors, at least 1 hour or up to 4 hours.

EACH SERVING: About 85 calories (21 percent calories from fat), 3g protein, 17g carbohydrate, 2g total fat (0g saturated), 4g fiber, 0mg cholesterol, 157mg sodium ♥ 📖

Crunchy Carrot Coleslaw

A mix of shredded cabbage and carrots gives this slaw its crunch; cider vinegar and a little cayenne give it a bite.

TOTAL TIME: 10 minutes

MAKES: 10 cups or 8 side-dish servings

⅓	cup fresh orange juice
¼	cup cider vinegar
2	tablespoons sugar
2	tablespoons Dijon mustard
1	tablespoon vegetable oil
1	teaspoon salt
¼	teaspoon dried mint
⅛	teaspoon cayenne (ground red) pepper
1	bag (16 ounces) shredded cabbage (for coleslaw)
1	bag (10 ounces) shredded carrots

In large bowl, with wire whisk, mix orange juice, vinegar, sugar, mustard, oil, salt, mint, and cayenne until blended. Add cabbage and carrots; toss well. Serve slaw at room temperature, or cover and refrigerate until ready to serve.

EACH SERVING: About 65 calories (28 percent calories from fat), 1g protein, 12g carbohydrate, 2g total fat (0g saturated), 2g fiber, 0mg cholesterol, 385mg sodium ♥ 📖

Korean Steak in Lettuce Cups

Sliced round steak and shredded carrots are braised in a rich soy-ginger sauce and served in delicate Boston-lettuce leaves.

ACTIVE TIME: 15 minutes
TOTAL TIME: 20 minutes plus marinating
MAKES: 4 main-dish servings

3	tablespoons soy sauce
1	tablespoon sugar
2	teaspoons Asian sesame oil
1	teaspoon minced, peeled fresh ginger
¼	teaspoon cayenne (ground red) pepper
1	garlic clove, crushed with garlic press
1	beef top round steak (about 1 pound), trimmed, cut into ½-inch cubes
4	celery stalks with leaves, thinly sliced
½	(10-ounce) package shredded carrots (1¾ cups)
3	green onions, thinly sliced
1	tablespoon sesame seeds, toasted (see Tip)
1	head Boston lettuce, separated into leaves

green-onion tops for garnish

1. In medium bowl, stir soy sauce, sugar, oil, ginger, cayenne, and garlic until blended. Add beef, turning to coat with soy-sauce mixture, and marinate 15 minutes at room temperature, stirring occasionally.

2. In 12-inch skillet, heat celery, carrots, and ½ cup water to boiling over medium-high heat. Cook 2 to 3 minutes or until vegetables are tender-crisp, stirring occasionally. Add beef with its marinade and cook 2 minutes or until meat just loses its pink color throughout, stirring quickly and constantly. Stir in green onions and sesame seeds; cook 1 minute, stirring.

3. To serve, let each person place some beef mixture on a lettuce leaf. Garnish with green-onion tops. If you like, fold sides of lettuce leaf over filling to make a package to eat out of hand.

EACH SERVING: About 300 calories (30 percent calories from fat), 28g protein, 12g carbohydrate, 10g total fat (3 g saturated), 3g fiber, 53mg cholesterol, 855mg sodium

TIP: *Toasting brings out the nutty flavor of sesame seeds. To toast, heat seeds in a small, dry skillet over medium heat, stirring constantly, until fragrant and a shade darker, 3 to 5 minutes.*

Warm Eggplant and Wheat-Berry Salad

This salad serves up a rainbow of goodness—vitamins A, C, B$_6$, and K (to name just a few), as well as iron, protein, and antioxidants galore.

ACTIVE TIME: 35 minutes
TOTAL TIME: 2 hours and 40 minutes plus soaking
MAKES: 4 main-dish servings

1   cup wheat berries (whole-wheat kernels)

6¾ cups water

1   can (14½ ounces) low-sodium vegetable broth or 1¾ cups homemade (page 56)

2   tablespoons olive oil

1   teaspoon salt

1   teaspoon dried thyme

½   teaspoon coarsely ground black pepper

1   medium yellow pepper, cut into ¼-inch-wide strips

1   small zucchini (about 8 ounces), halved lengthwise and cut into ¾-inch chunks

1   package (8 ounces) mushrooms, each cut in half

1   small eggplant (about 12 ounces), cut lengthwise into quarters and sliced into ¾-inch chunks

1   cup frozen peas, thawed

1   small ripe tomato, cut into ½-inch chunks

1. In large bowl, soak wheat berries overnight in 5 cups water.

2. Drain wheat berries. In 2-quart saucepan over high heat, heat wheat berries, broth, and remaining 1¾ cups water to boiling over high heat. Reduce heat to low; cover and simmer until wheat berries are tender, about 2½ hours.

3. After wheat berries have cooked 1½ hours, preheat broiler as manufacturer directs.

4. Coat rack in broiling pan with nonstick cooking spray. In medium bowl, mix 1 tablespoon oil, ½ teaspoon salt, ½ teaspoon thyme, and ¼ teaspoon black pepper; add yellow pepper, zucchini, and mushrooms, tossing to coat. Arrange vegetables on rack in broiling pan. Place pan under broiler 5 to 7 inches from source of heat; broil vegetables until tender and browned, 10 to 15 minutes, stirring them occasionally and removing them to large bowl as they are done. Keep vegetables warm.

5. In same medium bowl, mix remaining 1 tablespoon oil, ½ teaspoon salt, ½ teaspoon thyme, and ¼ teaspoon pepper; add eggplant, tossing to coat. Arrange eggplant on rack in broiling pan; broil until tender and browned, 10 to 15 minutes, stirring occasionally. Remove to bowl with other vegetables.

6. About 5 minutes before end of wheat berry cooking time, add thawed peas to heat through. Drain any liquid from wheat-berry mixture. Add wheat berries and tomato chunks to bowl with vegetables; toss to mix well. Serve warm.

EACH SERVING: About 315 calories (23 percent calories from fat), 13g protein, 50g carbohydrate, 8g total fat (1g saturated), 12g fiber, 0mg cholesterol, 650mg sodium ♥

Warm Farro Salad with Roasted Vegetables

If you've never tried farro, this hearty main-dish salad is the perfect opportunity to enjoy its nutty goodness. Try it as a side dish alongside grilled fish or chicken, or serve on a bed of lettuce for a main dish.

ACTIVE TIME: 25 minutes
TOTAL TIME: 1 hour 5 minutes
MAKES: 6 side-dish servings

2	large carrots, peeled and cut into ½-inch dice
2	small fennel bulbs, trimmed and cut into 1-inch pieces
1	red onion, halved and sliced through root end
3	tablespoons olive oil
1	teaspoon salt
¼	teaspoon ground black pepper
1	bunch radishes, cut into ½-inch dice
1	tablespoon red wine vinegar
2½ cups water	
1	cup farro
3	tablespoons fresh lemon juice
2	teaspoons freshly grated lemon peel
1	cup lightly packed fresh basil leaves, chopped

1. Preheat oven to 400°F.

2. In large bowl, combine carrots, fennel, red onion, 1 tablespoon oil, ½ teaspoon salt, and ⅛ teaspoon pepper; toss. Turn onto 15½" by 10½" jelly-roll pan and spread evenly. Roast 20 minutes, stirring once. Stir in radishes and roast until vegetables are tender, about 10 minutes. Stir in vinegar.

3. Meanwhile, in medium saucepan, bring water, farro, and ¼ teaspoon salt to boiling over high heat. Reduce heat to medium-low; cover and simmer until farro is tender and water is absorbed, 25 to 30 minutes.

4. In large bowl, whisk lemon juice, lemon peel, remaining 2 tablespoons oil, ¼ teaspoon salt, and ⅛ teaspoon pepper. Add farro, roasted vegetables, and basil; toss to combine. Serve warm.

EACH SERVING: About 215 calories (29 percent calories from fat), 6g protein, 34g carbohydrate, 7g total fat (1g saturated), 6g fiber, 0mg cholesterol, 472mg sodium ✿

GET YOUR GRAINS: FARRO

This ancient grain is also known as emmer wheat. It contains starch that is similar to the starch found in short-grain rices; try substituting it for Arborio rice the next time you make risotto. A good source of fiber and protein, farro has a nutty wheat flavor and chewy texture.

Barley, Corn, and Tomato Salad

Here the whole-grain goodness of pearl barley is combined with the fresh flavors of summer—corn cut from the cob, tomatoes off the vine, and the heady perfume of basil.

ACTIVE TIME: 15 minutes
TOTAL TIME: 40 minutes

MAKES: 12 side-dish servings

2½ cups water

1¼ cups pearl barley

5 medium ears corn, husks and silk removed

1 small bunch fresh basil

¼ cup rice vinegar

3 tablespoons olive oil

1 teaspoon salt

¼ teaspoon ground black pepper

2 large ripe tomatoes (about 8 ounces each), cut into ½-inch chunks

2 green onions

1. In 2-quart saucepan, heat water to boiling over high heat. Stir in barley; return to boiling. Reduce heat to low; cover and simmer until barley is tender, 30 to 35 minutes.

2. Meanwhile, place corn on plate in microwave. Cook on High 4 to 5 minutes, turning and rearranging corn halfway through cooking. Cool slightly until easy to handle. Chop enough basil leaves to equal ⅓ cup; reserve remaining basil for garnish.

3. With sharp knife, cut corn kernels from cobs. In large bowl, with fork, mix vinegar, oil, salt, and pepper; stir in corn, warm barley, tomatoes, green onions, and chopped basil until combined. If not serving right away, cover and refrigerate up to 4 hours. Garnish with basil leaves.

EACH SERVING: About 145 calories (25 percent calories from fat), 4g protein, 26g carbohydrate, 4g total fat (1g saturated), 5g fiber, 0mg cholesterol, 205mg sodium ♥ ☺ ▤

GET YOUR GRAINS: BARLEY

Barley is one of the oldest grains in cultivation. In most grains, the fiber is concentrated in the bran, which is removed when the kernel is refined. But even when all of barley's tough bran is removed (as with pearl barley, the most refined type), at least half the original fiber remains. A half cup of cooked barley contains 3 grams of fiber, compared to white rice's one-third gram.

Snap Pea Salad

This yummy double-pea salad is easy to prepare and pretty to serve. Use any leftover fresh dill in your next mayonnaise-based salad.

ACTIVE TIME: 10 minutes
TOTAL TIME: 15 minutes
MAKES: 8 side-dish servings

1	pound sugar snap peas, strings removed
1	package (10 ounces) frozen peas
½	cup minced red onion
2	tablespoons white wine vinegar
2	tablespoons vegetable oil
2	tablespoons chopped fresh dill
1	tablespoon sugar
½	teaspoon salt
¼	teaspoon coarsely ground black pepper

1. In 5- to 6-quart saucepot, heat *2 inches water* to boiling over high heat. Add snap peas and frozen peas; cook 1 minute. Drain peas; rinse under cold running water to stop cooking. Drain again; pat dry between layers of paper towels.

2. In large bowl, stir onion, vinegar, oil, dill, sugar, salt, and pepper until mixed. Add peas; toss to coat. If not serving right away, cover and refrigerate up to 4 hours.

EACH SERVING: About 100 calories (27 percent calories from fat), 4g protein, 13g carbohydrate, 3g total fat (0g saturated), 4g fiber, 0mg cholesterol, 245mg sodium 🟢 ❤️ 🍽️

Zesty Potato Salad

Spicy mustard, onion, and cider vinegar lend this salad zip; light mayo keeps it skinny.

ACTIVE TIME: 15 minutes
TOTAL TIME: 30 minutes plus standing and chilling
MAKES: 6 cups or 10 side-dish servings

2	pounds red potatoes (about 8 medium), cut into 1-inch chunks
¼	cup minced onion
3	tablespoons cider vinegar
2	teaspoons spicy brown mustard
1	teaspoon salt
½	teaspoon ground black pepper
⅓	cup light mayonnaise
¼	cup low-fat (1%) milk
1	large stalk celery, finely chopped
½	cup loosely packed fresh parsley leaves, chopped

1. In 4-quart saucepan, place potatoes and enough *water* to cover by 1 inch; heat to boiling over high heat. Reduce heat and simmer 6 to 7 minutes or until potatoes are tender. Meanwhile, in large bowl, with whisk, mix onion, vinegar, mustard, salt, and pepper.

2. Drain potatoes well; add to dressing in bowl and gently stir with rubber spatula until evenly coated. Let stand 20 minutes to cool slightly.

3. In small bowl, whisk mayonnaise and milk. Add mayonnaise mixture, celery, and parsley to potato mixture; gently stir with rubber spatula until potatoes are well coated. If not serving right away, cover and refrigerate up to 1 day.

EACH SERVING: About 110 calories (23 percent calories from fat), 3g protein, 18g carbohydrate, 3g total fat (0g saturated), 1g fiber, 3mg cholesterol, 321mg sodium ❤️ 🍽️

Three-Bean Tuna Salad

This no-cook salad serves up heart-healthy omega-3 fats (the tuna) and nearly three-quarters of a day's worth of cholesterol-lowering fiber (the beans).

TOTAL TIME: 15 minutes

MAKES: 6 main-dish servings

1	lemon
2	tablespoons extra-virgin olive oil
3	stalks celery, thinly sliced
2	green onions, thinly sliced
¼	teaspoon salt
⅛	teaspoon coarsely ground black pepper
3	cans (15 to 19 ounces each) assorted low-sodium beans such as white kidney beans (cannellini), garbanzo beans, and pink beans, rinsed and drained
2	cans (6 ounces each) chunk light tuna in water, drained and coarsely flaked
6	large Boston lettuce leaves

1. From lemon, grate 1 teaspoon peel and squeeze 2 tablespoons juice.

2. In large bowl, mix lemon peel and juice, oil, celery, green onions, salt, and pepper. Stir in beans until coated, then gently stir in tuna.

3. Serve bean mixture in lettuce cups.

EACH SERVING: About 335 calories (19 percent calories from fat), 25g protein, 42g carbohydrate, 7g total fat (1g saturated), 11g fiber, 29mg cholesterol, 517mg sodium 🌿 🌾

Chilled Tuscan-Style Tomato Soup

The lush summer flavors of Tuscany shine in this refreshing, easy-to-make cold tomato soup. We blend cubes of country bread in with the tomatoes, to achieve a thicker body and a velvety mouthfeel. For photo, see page 10.

TOTAL TIME: 15 minutes plus chilling

MAKES: 6 cups or 4 first-course servings

1	teaspoon olive oil
1	garlic clove, minced
2	cups cubed country-style bread (1-inch cubes; 3 ounces)
3	pounds ripe tomatoes, each cut into quarters
¼	cup loosely packed fresh basil leaves, chopped, plus additional basil leaves, for garnish
1	teaspoon sugar
½	teaspoon salt

1. In small skillet, heat oil over medium heat until hot. Add garlic and cook 1 minute, stirring. Remove skillet from heat.

2. In food processor with knife blade attached, pulse bread until coarsely chopped. Add tomatoes and garlic; pulse until soup is almost pureed. Pour soup into bowl; stir in chopped basil, sugar, and salt. Cover and refrigerate until well chilled, at least 2 hours or overnight. Garnish each serving with basil leaves.

EACH SERVING: About 145 calories (19 percent calories from fat), 5g protein, 28g carbohydrate, 3g total fat (1g saturated), 4g fiber, 0mg cholesterol, 445mg sodium 🍲

Chilled Buttermilk and Corn Soup

This refreshing refrigerator soup—with corn, tomatoes, cucumber, and basil—is both low in fat and satisfying.

TOTAL TIME: 20 minutes plus chilling

MAKES: 4½ cups or 6 first-course servings

1	quart buttermilk
4	ripe medium tomatoes (1½ pounds), seeded and chopped
1	small cucumber, peeled, seeded, and chopped
2	cups corn kernels cut from cobs (about 4 ears)
½	teaspoon salt
¼	teaspoon coarsely ground black pepper
10	fresh basil sprigs

1. In large bowl, combine buttermilk, tomatoes, cucumber, corn, salt, and pepper. Cover and refrigerate until very cold, at least 2 hours.

2. To serve, set aside 6 small basil sprigs; pinch 12 large basil leaves from remaining sprigs and thinly slice. Spoon soup into bowls; garnish with sliced basil and small basil sprigs.

EACH SERVING: About 135 calories (13 percent calories from fat), 8g protein, 24g carbohydrate, 2g total fat (1g saturated), 2g fiber, 6mg cholesterol, 365mg sodium 🍲

Carrot and Dill Soup

Combine sweet carrots with fresh orange, dill, and a touch of milk for a refreshing, creamy soup without the cream.

ACTIVE TIME: 25 minutes
TOTAL TIME: 1 hour 10 minutes

MAKES: 10½ cups or 10 first-course servings

1	tablespoon olive oil
1	large onion (12 ounces), chopped
1	stalk celery, chopped
2	large oranges
2	bags (16 ounces each) carrots, peeled and chopped
1	can (14½ ounces) vegetable broth or 1¾ cups homemade (page 56)
1	tablespoon sugar
¾	teaspoon salt
¼	teaspoon coarsely ground black pepper
4	cups water
1	cup milk
¼	cup chopped fresh dill
	dill sprigs for garnish

1. In 5-quart Dutch oven, heat oil over medium-high heat. Add onion and celery; cook until tender and golden, about 15 minutes, stirring occasionally.

2. Meanwhile, with vegetable peeler, remove 4 strips of peel (3" by 1" each) from oranges and squeeze 1 cup juice.

3. Add orange-peel strips to Dutch oven and cook 2 minutes longer, stirring. Add orange juice, carrots, broth, sugar, salt, pepper, and water; heat to boiling over high heat. Reduce heat to low; cover and simmer until carrots are very tender, about 25 minutes.

4. Remove strips of orange peel from soup. In blender, with center part of lid removed to allow steam to escape, blend soup in small batches until smooth. Pour pureed soup into large bowl after each batch.

5. Return soup to Dutch oven; stir in milk and chopped dill; heat just to simmering over medium heat. Spoon soup into bowls; garnish each serving with dill sprigs.

EACH SERVING: About 95 calories (28 percent calories from fat), 3g protein, 16g carbohydrate, 3g total fat (1g saturated), 3g fiber, 3mg cholesterol, 335mg sodium ♥

THE SKINNY ON SOUP

Looking to lose a few pounds? Embrace soup. Research shows that the best way to start a meal may be with a broth- or water-based soup. It fills you up—even more so than salad or other low-calorie foods—so you'll end up eating less at that meal.

Or make soup a meal in itself. Try our veggie- and grain-based soups; they provide fiber to keep you feeling fuller longer. Look for this icon 🌱 to locate soup recipes that are high in fiber, containing 5 grams or more of fiber per serving.

Barley Minestrone with Pesto

Top this soup with a dollop of our homemade pesto, which you can make in a mini food processor or blender. In a hurry? Store-bought refrigerated pesto makes an excellent stand-in— although it's not as light as our version. For photo, see page 15.

ACTIVE TIME: 50 minutes
TOTAL TIME: 1 hour 15 minutes

MAKES: 10 ½ cups or 6 main-dish servings

MINESTRONE

1	cup pearl barley
1	tablespoon olive oil
2	cups thinly sliced green cabbage (about ¼ small head)
2	large carrots, peeled, each cut lengthwise in half, then crosswise into ½-inch-thick slices
2	large stalks celery, cut into ½-inch dice
1	onion, cut into ½-inch dice
1	garlic clove, finely chopped
3	cups water
2	cans (14½ ounces each) vegetable broth or 3½ cups homemade (page 56)
1	can (14½ ounces) diced tomatoes
¼	teaspoon salt
1	medium zucchini (8 to 10 ounces), cut into ½-inch dice
4	ounces green beans, trimmed and cut into ½-inch pieces (1 cup)

LIGHT PESTO

1	cup firmly packed fresh basil leaves
2	tablespoons olive oil
2	tablespoons water
¼	teaspoon salt
¼	cup freshly grated Pecorino-Romano cheese
1	garlic clove, finely chopped

1. Heat 5- to 6-quart Dutch oven over medium-high until hot. Add barley and cook until toasted and fragrant, 3 to 4 minutes, stirring constantly. Transfer barley to small bowl; set aside.

2. Add oil to same Dutch oven, still over medium-high heat. When oil is hot, add cabbage, carrots, celery, and onion; cook until vegetables are tender and lightly browned, 8 to 10 minutes, stirring occasionally. Add garlic and cook until fragrant, 30 seconds. Stir in barley, water, broth, tomatoes with their juice, and salt. Cover and heat to boiling over high heat. Reduce heat to low and simmer 25 minutes.

3. Stir zucchini and green beans into barley mixture; increase heat to medium, cover, and cook until all vegetables are barely tender, 10 to 15 minutes longer.

4. Meanwhile, prepare pesto: In blender container with narrow base or in mini food processor, combine basil, oil, water, and salt; cover and blend until mixture is pureed. Transfer pesto to small bowl; stir in Romano and garlic. Makes about ½ cup pesto.

5. Ladle minestrone into six large soup bowls. Top each serving with some pesto.

EACH SERVING SOUP WITH 1 TEASPOON PESTO: About 230 calories (20 percent calories from fat), 7g protein, 42g carbohydrate, 5g total fat (0g saturated), 9g fiber, 1mg cholesterol, 725mg sodium

Black-Bean Soup

This simple but hearty soup is sure to become a standby. The cilantro and fresh lime juice add Latin flavor.

ACTIVE TIME: 15 minutes
TOTAL TIME: 45 minutes plus cooling
MAKES: 6½ cups or 6 main-dish servings

1	tablespoon olive oil
2	medium carrots, peeled and chopped
2	garlic cloves, finely chopped
1	large onion (10 to 12 ounces), chopped
1	medium red pepper (4 to 6 ounces), chopped
2	teaspoons ground cumin
¼	teaspoon crushed red pepper
½	teaspoon salt
2	cups water
2	cans black beans (15 to 19 ounces), rinsed and drained
1	can (14½ ounces) reduced-sodium chicken broth
¼	cup fresh cilantro leaves, chopped, plus sprigs for garnish
1	tablespoon fresh lime juice

EAT YOUR BEANS

Whether you choose black beans, garbanzos, pintos, or cannellini, beans are packed with protein and insoluble and soluble fiber. Insoluble fiber helps promote regularity and may stave off such digestive disorders as diverticulosis. Soluble fiber can reduce LDL cholesterol levels and help control blood-sugar levels in people with diabetes. Beans are also high in saponin, a cancer-fighting plant compound.

1. In 6-quart saucepot, heat oil over medium heat until hot. Add carrots, garlic, onion, and pepper; cook 12 to 15 minutes or until vegetables are lightly browned and tender, stirring occasionally. Add cumin, crushed red pepper, and salt; cook 1 minute.

2. Stir in water, beans, and broth; heat to boiling over medium-high heat. Reduce heat to low and simmer, uncovered, 15 minutes to blend flavors.

3. Ladle 3 cups soup into blender; cover, with center part of lid removed to allow steam to escape, and blend until pureed. Stir puree into soup in saucepot; heat through over medium heat. Stir in cilantro and lime juice, and garnish with cilantro sprigs to serve.

EACH SERVING: About 165 calories (16 percent calories from fat), 9g protein, 33g carbohydrate, 3g total fat (0g saturated), 11g fiber, 0mg cholesterol, 705mg sodium 🌱 🍱

Hearty Fish Chowder

Cod, potatoes, and a sprinkling of crumbled bacon make every bite of this creamy chowder rich and satisfying.

ACTIVE TIME: 20 minutes
TOTAL TIME: 35 minutes

MAKES: 4 main-dish servings

4	slices center-cut bacon
1	large carrot, peeled and chopped
1	medium celery root (13 ounces), peeled and chopped
1	large all-purpose potato (12 ounces), peeled and chopped
2	tablespoons plus ½ cup water
2	small onions (4 to 6 ounces each), chopped
2	tablespoons all-purpose flour
1	cup bottled clam juice
1	pound skinless cod fillets, cut into 1-inch chunks
½	cup reduced-fat (2%) milk
¼	teaspoon salt
⅛	teaspoon freshly ground black pepper

fresh flat-leaf parsley leaves, chopped,
    for garnish

1. In 6- to 7-quart saucepot, cook bacon over medium heat 5 to 7 minutes or until browned and crisp, turning occasionally. Drain on paper towels; set aside. Discard all but 1 tablespoon bacon fat. Keep saucepot with rendered bacon fat over medium heat.

2. While bacon cooks, in large microwave-safe bowl, combine carrot, celery root, potato, and 2 tablespoons water. Cover with vented plastic wrap and microwave on High 5 minutes or until vegetables are just tender.

3. Add onion to saucepot and cook 6 to 8 minutes or until tender, stirring occasionally. Add carrot mixture and cook 2 minutes, stirring.

4. Add flour and cook 2 minutes, stirring. Add clam juice and remaining ½ cup water and whisk until smooth. Heat to boiling, stirring occasionally. Add cod chunks, cover, and cook 4 to 5 minutes or until fish just turns opaque throughout.

5. Stir in milk, salt, and pepper. Cook 1 to 2 minutes or until hot but not boiling. Spoon chowder into shallow bowls; sprinkle with parsley and crumble 1 strip bacon over each serving.

EACH SERVING: About 310 calories (20 percent calories from fat), 27g protein, 35g carbohydrate, 7g total fat (3g saturated), 5g fiber, 64mg cholesterol, 595mg sodium 🌼

Quick Cream of Asparagus Soup

Start with a package of frozen vegetables, a can of broth, and seasonings—in 25 minutes you'll have a luscious, creamy, lower-fat soup.

ACTIVE TIME: 5 minutes
TOTAL TIME: 25 minutes

MAKES: 3¾ cups or 4 first-course servings

1	tablespoon butter or margarine
1	onion, finely chopped
1	can (14½ ounces) fat-free chicken broth
1	package (10 ounces) frozen asparagus cuts or spears
¼	teaspoon dried thyme
¼	teaspoon dried tarragon
⅛	teaspoon salt
⅛	teaspoon ground black pepper
1½	cups skim milk
2	teaspoons fresh lemon juice
	snipped fresh chives for garnish (optional)

1. In 2-quart saucepan, melt butter over medium heat. Add onion and cook, stirring occasionally, until tender, 5 minutes. Add broth, asparagus, thyme, tarragon, salt, and pepper; heat to boiling over high heat. Reduce heat to low and simmer 10 minutes.

2. Spoon one-fourth of mixture into blender; cover, with center part of lid removed to let steam escape, and puree until smooth. Pour puree into bowl. Repeat with remaining mixture.

3. Return soup to saucepan; stir in milk. Heat through over medium heat, stirring often (do not boil, or soup may curdle). Remove saucepan from heat; stir in lemon juice. Garnish with snipped chives, if you like.

EACH SERVING: About 115 calories (24 percent calories from fat), 8g protein, 11g carbohydrate, 3g total fat (1g saturated), 2g fiber, 2mg cholesterol, 480mg sodium ⊘

QUICK CREAM OF CAULIFLOWER SOUP: Prepare as directed but substitute *1 package (10 ounces) frozen cauliflower florets* for asparagus and *½ teaspoon curry powder* for dried tarragon. If you like, garnish with *chopped fresh apple.*

EACH SERVING: About 115 calories (24 percent calories from fat), 8g protein, 11g carbohydrate, 3g total fat (1g saturated), 2g fiber, 2mg cholesterol, 480mg sodium ⊘

QUICK CREAM OF SQUASH SOUP: Prepare as directed but substitute *1 package (10 ounces) frozen winter squash* for asparagus. Add *¼ teaspoon pumpkin-pie spice* to onions at the end of cooking time and cook 30 seconds longer. Omit dried tarragon. If you like, garnish with *chopped ripe tomato.*

EACH SERVING: About 115 calories (23 percent calories from fat), 8g protein, 11g carbohydrate, 3g total fat (1g saturated), 2g fiber, 2mg cholesterol, 480mg sodium ⊘

Classic Beef Stew

Lean beef, winter vegetables, and a richly flavored sauce make this a candidate for family suppers or casual entertaining.

ACTIVE TIME: 30 minutes
TOTAL TIME: 1 hour 30 minutes
MAKES: 6 main-dish servings

1	pound lean beef for stew, trimmed and cut into 1-inch cubes
1	tablespoon vegetable oil
½	teaspoon salt
2	stalks celery, chopped
1	large onion (12 ounces), chopped
1	can (14½ ounces) stewed tomatoes
1	can (14½ ounces) beef broth
1	cup plus 2 tablespoons water
3	large potatoes (1½ pounds), peeled and cut into 1½-inch chunks
3	medium carrots (8 ounces), peeled and cut into ¾-inch chunks
3	medium turnips (12 ounces), peeled and cut into 1½-inch chunks
1	tablespoon soy sauce
2	tablespoons all-purpose flour
1	package (10 ounces) frozen peas
2	tablespoons freshly grated lemon peel

1. Pat beef dry with paper towels. In 5-quart Dutch oven, heat oil over medium-high heat until very hot. Add beef, sprinkle with salt, and cook, turning pieces occasionally, until beef is browned on all sides. Transfer beef to bowl.

2. Add celery and onion to drippings in Dutch oven and cook, stirring, until lightly browned. Return beef to Dutch oven; stir in stewed tomatoes, broth, and 1 cup water. Heat to boiling over high heat. Reduce heat to low; cover and simmer 25 minutes.

3. Add potatoes, carrots, turnips, and soy sauce; heat to boiling over high heat. Reduce heat to low; cover and simmer until meat and vegetables in pot are fork-tender, about 20 minutes longer.

4. In cup, with fork, mix flour and remaining 2 tablespoons water until blended. Stir flour mixture into meat mixture; cook over medium-high heat until mixture boils and thickens slightly. Stir in frozen peas; heat through. Sprinkle with lemon peel.

EACH SERVING: About 330 calories (19 percent calories from fat), 23g protein, 45g carbohydrate, 7g total fat (2g saturated), 7g fiber, 53mg cholesterol, 905mg sodium 🌱 🍲

Valentine's Day Red Chili

Beets and fire-roasted tomatoes color this delicious vegetarian chili—and provide the inspiration for its name.

ACTIVE TIME: 35 minutes
TOTAL TIME: 1 hour 30 minutes
MAKES: 9 cups or 6 main-dish servings

2	teaspoons ground cumin
1	teaspoon dried oregano
½	teaspoon chipotle chile powder
2	tablespoons vegetable oil
3	large beets (6 to 8 ounces each), trimmed, peeled, and chopped
1	jumbo red onion (1 pound), finely chopped
1	large red pepper (8 to 10 ounces), chopped
½	teaspoon ground black pepper
4	garlic cloves, crushed with press
1	can (28 ounces) fire-roasted diced tomatoes
1	can (15 ounces) low-sodium black beans, rinsed and drained
1	can (15 ounces) low-sodium red kidney beans, rinsed and drained
1	can (15 ounces) low-sodium pinto beans, rinsed and drained
1	cup water
1	cup reduced-fat sour cream
¼	cup fresh cilantro leaves

1. In 7- to 8-quart Dutch oven or heavy saucepot, combine cumin, oregano, and chile powder. Cook over medium heat 1 to 2 minutes or until toasted and fragrant. Transfer to sheet of waxed paper; set aside. In same Dutch oven, heat oil over medium heat until hot. Add beets, onion, red pepper, and ¼ teaspoon black pepper. Cook 15 minutes or until vegetables are tender, stirring occasionally.

2. Add garlic and reserved spice mixture. Cook 2 minutes, stirring constantly. Add tomatoes, all beans, and water. Heat to boiling over medium-high heat. Reduce heat to medium-low and simmer 30 minutes, stirring and mashing some beans occasionally. Season with remaining ¼ teaspoon black pepper. (Can be prepared up to this point up to 2 days ahead; transfer to airtight container and refrigerate. Reheat before serving.) Divide among serving bowls and top with sour cream and cilantro.

EACH SERVING: About 345 calories (29 percent calories from fat), 15g protein, 52g carbohydrate, 10g total fat (3g saturated), 15g fiber, 13mg cholesterol, 540mg sodium 🌱 📦

Turkey and White Bean Chili

You can cut calories by a third and fat by half when you substitute ground turkey for beef chuck. The cannellini beans deliver an impressive 10 grams of fiber per serving— almost half your daily requirement.

ACTIVE TIME: 15 minutes
TOTAL TIME: 25 minutes

MAKES: 6 cups or 4 main-dish servings

1	tablespoon olive oil
1	pound ground turkey (93% lean)
½	teaspoon salt
1	onion, chopped
4	teaspoon chili powder
1	tablespoon ground cumin
1	can (28 ounces) whole tomatoes in juice, chopped
1	can (15 to 19 ounces) white kidney beans (cannellini), rinsed and drained
½	cup water
½	cup plain nonfat yogurt

1. In 12-inch skillet, heat oil over medium-high heat until hot. Add turkey and salt, and cook 6 to 8 minutes or until turkey loses its pink color throughout, stirring to break meat up with side of spoon. Add onion and cook 4 minutes. Stir in chili powder and cumin; cook 1 minute.

2. Add tomatoes with their juice, beans, and water; heat to boiling over high heat. Reduce heat to medium and cook, uncovered, 10 minutes, stirring occasionally. Ladle chili into serving bowls and top with a dollop of yogurt.

EACH SERVING: About 380 calories (30 percent calories from fat), 33g protein, 35g carbohydrate, 13g total fat (3g saturated), 10g fiber, 81mg cholesterol, 875mg sodium 💚 🌱 🍽

South-of-the-Border Chicken Soup

We give this rich chicken soup a Latin accent with lime and cilantro. Serve it with chunks of avocado and baked tortilla chips, if desired.

ACTIVE TIME: 25 minutes
TOTAL TIME: 1 hour 25 minutes
MAKES: 16 cups or 8 main-dish servings

8	medium all-purpose potatoes (2½ pounds)
1	chicken (4 pounds), cut into 8 pieces
3	large stalks celery, each cut into thirds
3	carrots, peeled and each cut into thirds
2	onions unpeeled, each cut into quarters
10	cups water
10	sprigs fresh cilantro, plus ¼ cup chopped
2	bay leaves
1	teaspoon whole black peppercorns
1	can (15¼ to 16 ounces) whole-kernel corn, drained
2	teaspoons salt
¼	cup fresh lime juice (3 large limes)
2	medium avocados, cut into ½-inch pieces
	baked tortilla chips and lime wedges (optional)

1. Peel 3 potatoes. In 8-quart Dutch oven, combine chicken, peeled potatoes, celery, carrots, onions, water, cilantro sprigs, bay leaves, and peppercorns; heat to boiling over high heat. Reduce heat; cover and simmer until chicken loses its pink color throughout and vegetables are tender, 35 to 45 minutes. Transfer chicken and potatoes to separate bowls.

2. Strain broth through sieve into large bowl; discard vegetables. Skim and discard fat from broth; clean Dutch oven and return broth to pot. Mash cooked potatoes with 1 cup broth; stir potato mixture into broth in Dutch oven.

3. Peel and chop remaining 5 potatoes. Add to broth; heat to boiling over high heat. Reduce heat; cover and simmer until potatoes are tender, about 10 minutes.

4. Meanwhile, discard skin and bones from chicken; cut chicken into bite-size pieces. Stir chicken, corn, and salt into broth; heat through.

5. Just before serving, stir lime juice and ¼ cup chopped cilantro into soup. Top with avocado and serve with tortilla chips and/or lime wedges, if you like.

EACH SERVING: About 345 calories (29 percent calories from fat), 28g protein, 34g carbohydrate, 11g total fat (2g saturated), 6g fiber, 76mg cholesterol, 772mg sodium

Homemade Vegetable Broth

This broth is delicious, nutritious, and great in soups, risottos, and sauces. The optional fennel and parsnip lend a natural sweetness and additional depth of flavor. For an Asian-flavored broth, add minced lemongrass, minced fresh ginger, or chopped fresh cilantro.

ACTIVE TIME: 25 minutes
TOTAL TIME: 2 hours 25 minutes
MAKES: 6 cups

4	large leeks
2 to 4	garlic cloves, not peeled
13	cups water
	salt
1	large all-purpose potato, peeled, cut lengthwise in half, and thinly sliced
1	small fennel bulb, trimmed and chopped (optional)
3	parsnips, peeled and thinly sliced (optional)
2	large carrots, peeled and thinly sliced
3	stalks celery with leaves, thinly sliced
4	ounces mushrooms, trimmed and thinly sliced
10	parsley sprigs
4	thyme sprigs
2	bay leaves
1	teaspoon whole black peppercorns, plus additional ground black pepper as needed

1. Cut off roots and trim dark green tops from leeks. Thinly slice leeks and rinse them in large bowl of cold water, swishing to remove sand. Transfer to colander to drain, leaving sand in bottom of bowl.

2. In 6-quart saucepot, combine leeks, garlic, 1 cup water, and pinch salt; heat to boiling. Reduce heat to medium; cover and cook until leeks are tender, about 15 minutes.

3. Add potato, fennel if using, parsnips if using, carrots, celery, mushrooms, parsley and thyme sprigs, bay leaves, peppercorns, and remaining 12 cups water. Heat to boiling; reduce heat and simmer, uncovered, at least 1 hour 30 minutes.

4. Taste and continue cooking if flavor is not concentrated enough. Season with salt and pepper to taste. Strain broth through fine-mesh sieve into containers, pressing on solids with back of wooden spoon to extract liquid; cool. Cover and refrigerate to use within 3 days, or freeze up to 4 months.

EACH CUP: About 20 calories (0 calories from fat), 1g protein, 4g carbohydrate, 0g total fat, 0mg cholesterol, 0g fiber, 9mg sodium ♥ ▥

Homemade Chicken Broth

Nothing beats the rich flavor of homemade chicken broth. It serves as a base for many of our soups and stews. Make large batches and freeze it in sturdy containers for up to four months. Bonus: The cooked chicken can be used in casseroles and salads.

ACTIVE TIME: 30 minutes
TOTAL TIME: 4 hours 40 minutes plus cooling
MAKES: 5½ cups

1	chicken (3 to 3½ pounds), including neck (reserve giblets for another use)
2	carrots, peeled and cut into 2-inch pieces
1	stalk celery, cut into 2-inch pieces
1	onion, unpeeled, cut into quarters
5	parsley sprigs
1	garlic clove, unpeeled
½	teaspoon dried thyme
½	bay leaf
3	quarts water plus more if needed

1. In 6-quart saucepot, combine chicken, chicken neck, carrots, celery, onion, parsley, garlic, thyme, bay leaf, and water. If necessary, add more water to cover broth ingredients; heat to boiling over high heat. With slotted spoon, skim foam from surface. Reduce heat to low; cover and simmer, turning chicken once and skimming foam occasionally, 1 hour.

2. Remove from heat; transfer chicken to large bowl. When chicken is cool enough to handle, remove skin and bones and reserve meat for another use. Return skin and bones to pot and return to boiling over high heat. Skim foam; reduce heat to low and simmer, uncovered, 3 hours.

3. Strain broth through colander into large bowl; discard solids. Strain again though fine-mesh sieve into containers; cool. Cover and refrigerate to use within 3 days, or freeze up to 4 months.

4. Discard fat from surface of chilled broth before use.

EACH CUP: About 35 calories (26 percent calories from fat), 3g protein, 4g carbohydrate, 1g total fat (1g saturated), 0g fiber, 3mg cholesterol, 91mg sodium ♥ ▆

Tuscan Tuna Salad Sandwiches

Tuna and cannellini beans are a popular combination in Italy. Tossed with a piquant dressing, it makes a great sandwich filling.

TOTAL TIME: 15 minutes

MAKES: 4 sandwiches

1	can (15 to 19 ounces) low-sodium white kidney beans (cannellini), rinsed and drained
½	cup chopped fresh basil
2	tablespoons capers, drained and chopped
2	tablespoons fresh lemon juice
2	tablespoons olive oil
½	teaspoon salt
¼	teaspoon coarsely ground black pepper
1	can (6 ounces) unsalted tuna packed in water, drained and flaked
1	bunch watercress (4 ounces), tough stems trimmed and sprigs cut in half
4	whole-wheat pita breads
2	ripe medium tomatoes (6 ounces each), thinly sliced

1. In large bowl, mash 1 cup beans. Stir in basil, capers, lemon juice, oil, salt, and pepper until well blended. Add tuna, watercress, and remaining beans; toss to mix.

2. Cut pita breads in half. Spoon tuna mixture onto pita halves; top with tomato slices.

EACH SANDWICH: About 330 calories (26 percent calories from fat), 20g protein, 44g carbohydrate, 10g total fat (1g saturated), 9g fiber, 15mg cholesterol, 724mg sodium ♥ ⚘

Curried Chicken Pitas

This curry-spiced chicken salad packs extra sweet flavor with the addition of cantaloupe.

TOTAL TIME: 20 minutes

MAKES: 4 sandwiches

¼	cup packed fresh cilantro leaves, finely chopped
¼	cup reduced-fat sour cream
2	tablespoons low-fat mayonnaise
1	tablespoon fresh lime juice
1	teaspoon grated, peeled fresh ginger
¼	teaspoon curry powder
¼	teaspoon ground coriander
⅛	teaspoon salt
2	cups chopped, cooked chicken-breast meat
5	radishes, cut into ¼-inch-thick half-moons
1½	cups chopped cantaloupe (8 ounces)
¼	small red onion, finely chopped
3	tablespoons roasted cashews, chopped
4	pita breads, toasted, each cut into quarters

1. In small bowl, whisk cilantro, sour cream, mayonnaise, lime juice, ginger, curry powder, coriander, and salt until well blended. If making ahead, cover and refrigerate up to 1 day.

2. In bowl, combine chicken, radishes, cantaloupe, and onion. If making ahead, cover and refrigerate up to 1 day. To serve, toss chicken mixture with half of dressing. Sprinkle with cashews. Spoon on top of pita pieces and serve with remaining dressing alongside.

EACH SANDWICH: About 380 calories (21 percent calories from fat), 29g protein, 45g carbohydrate, 9g total fat (3g saturated), 3g fiber, 65mg cholesterol, 535mg sodium ♥ ▨

Peking Chicken Roll-Ups

The traditional Chinese recipe for Peking duck is labor-intensive and takes several days to make. Our version, prepared in minutes, is made with grilled boneless chicken thighs and served in flour tortillas with hoisin sauce.

ACTIVE TIME: 25 minutes
TOTAL TIME: 35 minutes

MAKES: 4 main-dish servings

8	(7-inch) low-fat, low-sodium flour tortillas
2	tablespoons honey
2	tablespoons reduced-sodium soy sauce
1	tablespoon grated, peeled fresh ginger
⅛	teaspoon cayenne (ground red) pepper
2	garlic cloves, crushed with garlic press
6	skinless, boneless chicken thighs (about 1¼ pounds)
1	teaspoon vegetable oil
¼	cup hoisin sauce
½	English (seedless) cucumber, cut into 2" by ¼" matchsticks
2	green onions, thinly sliced

1. Prepare outdoor grill for direct grilling over medium-high heat.

2. Stack tortillas and wrap in foil. In small bowl, mix honey, soy sauce, ginger, cayenne, and garlic. Set aside tortillas and honey mixture.

3. Coat chicken with oil and place on hot grill rack over medium-high heat. Grill, turning once, 5 minutes. Brush chicken all over with honey mixture and grill until juices run clear when thickest part of thigh is pierced with tip of knife, 5 to 7 minutes longer, turning over once.

4. While chicken is cooking, place foil-wrapped tortillas on same grill rack and heat until warm, 3 to 5 minutes.

5. Transfer chicken to cutting board and thinly slice. Spread hoisin sauce on one side of each tortilla. Top with chicken, cucumber, and green onions; roll up to serve.

EACH SERVING: About 260 calories (26 percent calories from fat), 35g protein, 65g carbohydrate, 15g total fat (4g saturated), 9g fiber, 93mg cholesterol, 853mg sodium 🌱

Turkey Meatball Pitas

No one need ever know these meatballs are made with turkey instead of beef.

ACTIVE TIME: 20 minutes
TOTAL TIME: 30 minutes
MAKES: 5 sandwiches

1	pound ground turkey
2	slices whole-grain bread, chopped
2	tablespoons grated onion
1	large egg white
1½	teaspoons ground cumin
1	teaspoon salt
3	tablespoons water
5	(6-inch) whole-wheat pita breads
½	large cucumber, peeled and cut into ¾-inch pieces
1	container (8 ounces) plain nonfat yogurt
2	tablespoons chopped fresh cilantro or 1 teaspoon dried mint
4	cups thinly sliced romaine lettuce

1. Preheat oven to 425°F. Coat 15 ½" by 10 ½" jelly-roll pan with nonstick cooking spray.

2. In large bowl, with hands, mix turkey, bread, onion, egg white, cumin, ¾ teaspoon salt, and water. Wetting hands for easier shaping, form turkey mixture into 25 meatballs. Place meatballs in prepared jelly-roll pan and bake until cooked through (meatballs will not brown), 12 to 15 minutes.

3. Cut about 1 inch from top of each pita; reserve cut-off pieces for another use. Wrap pitas in foil. After meatballs have baked about 10 minutes, warm pitas in oven until meatballs are done.

4. Meanwhile, in small bowl, mix cucumber, yogurt, cilantro, and remaining ¼ teaspoon salt.

5. To serve, fill pitas with lettuce and meatballs; top with cucumber sauce.

EACH SANDWICH: About 380 calories (26 percent calories from fat), 28g protein, 44g carbohydrate, 11g total fat (3g saturated), 5g fiber, 46mg cholesterol, 909mg sodium ♥ ✿

EAT YOUR ONIONS

They may make you weep at the cutting board, but onions (and their brethren, leeks, shallots, and garlic, known as alliums) contain sulfur compounds that account for their distinctive flavor and aroma—and their nutritional benefits. They can inhibit the formation of blood clots and reduce the body's production of cholesterol. Studies suggest they may also defend against bacteria, fungi, viruses, and parasites.

Roast Beef Waldorf Sandwiches

Horseradish dressing and a crunchy celery-and-apple mixture make rare roast beef taste even better. Soaking the onions in ice water crisps them and tames their bite.

TOTAL TIME: 20 minutes plus standing

MAKES: 4 sandwiches

4	very thin slices red onion
½	Golden Delicious apple, peeled and finely chopped (½ cup)
2	stalks celery, finely chopped
4	tablespoons low-fat mayonnaise
2	tablespoons sour cream
½	teaspoon fresh lemon juice
1	tablespoon bottled white horseradish
8	slices pumpernickel bread, lightly toasted, if desired
8	ounces thinly sliced rare roast beef
1	bunch watercress (4 ounces), tough stems trimmed

1. In small bowl, combine onion with enough *ice water* to cover; let stand 15 minutes. Drain.

2. In separate small bowl, combine apple, celery, 2 tablespoons mayonnaise, 1 tablespoon sour cream, and lemon juice until well blended. In cup, combine remaining 2 tablespoons mayonnaise, remaining 1 tablespoon sour cream, and horseradish until blended.

3. Spread horseradish mixture evenly on 4 bread slices. Layer roast beef, onion, and watercress on top. Spread celery mixture evenly on remaining 4 bread slices and invert onto sandwiches. To serve, cut sandwiches in half.

EACH SANDWICH: About 295 calories (20 percent calories from fat), 22g protein, 40g carbohydrate, 7g total fat (3g saturated), 5g fiber, 31mg cholesterol, 726mg sodium

Steak Sandwiches with Grilled Onions

Marinating the steak with a delicious blend of Asian flavors and grilling it takes this classic sandwich to a new level.

ACTIVE TIME: 15 minutes
TOTAL TIME: 30 minutes plus marinating
MAKES: 4 main-dish servings

¼	cup reduced-sodium soy sauce
¼	cup balsamic vinegar
1	tablespoon brown sugar
1	teaspoon fresh thyme leaves
¼	teaspoon ground black pepper
1	beef flank steak (about 1¼ pounds)
1	(12-inch) metal skewer
1	medium red onion (about 8 ounces), cut into 4 thick slices
8	slices sourdough bread, toasted on grill, if you like
2	ripe medium tomatoes (6 to 8 ounces each), sliced
1	bunch (5 ounces) arugula, trimmed

1. In large zip-tight plastic bag, mix soy sauce, vinegar, brown sugar, thyme, and pepper. Add steak, turning to coat. Seal bag, pressing out excess air. Place bag on plate; let marinate 15 minutes at room temperature or 1 hour in the refrigerator, turning several times.

2. Prepare outdoor grill for covered direct grilling over medium heat.

3. Meanwhile, for easier handling, insert skewer horizontally through onion slices; set aside.

4. Remove steak from marinade; pour marinade into 1-quart saucepan. Heat marinade over high heat to boiling; boil 2 minutes.

5. Place steak and onion slices on hot grill rack over medium heat. Cover grill and cook steak and onions, brushing both with marinade occasionally and turning over once, until onions are browned and tender and meat is medium-rare, 12 to 15 minutes. Transfer steak to cutting board; let stand 10 minutes to allow juices to set for easier slicing. Separate onion into rings.

6. Thinly slice steak diagonally across grain. Arrange onion rings and steak on 4 slices of bread; spoon any meat juices from board over onion and steak. Top with tomatoes, arugula, and remaining slices of bread.

EACH SERVING: About 450 calories (20 percent calories from fat), 40g protein, 51g carbohydrate, 10g total fat (4g saturated), 4g fiber, 84mg cholesterol, 802mg sodium

Barbecue Pork Sandwiches

Good news: These little sandwiches allow you to partake in the barbecue, too. Round out your meal with a big green salad tossed with skinny Buttermilk-Chive Dressing (page 34).

ACTIVE TIME: 10 minutes
TOTAL TIME: 30 minutes

MAKES: 6 main-dish servings

3	tablespoons light molasses
3	tablespoons ketchup
1	tablespoon Worcestershire sauce
1	teaspoon minced, peeled fresh ginger
½	teaspoon grated lemon peel
1	garlic clove, crushed with garlic press
2	whole pork tenderloins (¾ pound each)
12	small, soft dinner rolls

1. Preheat broiler. In medium bowl, combine molasses, ketchup, Worcestershire, ginger, lemon peel, and garlic; add pork, turning to coat.

2. Place pork tenderloins on rack in broiling pan. Spoon any remaining molasses mixture over pork. Place pan in broiler 5 to 7 inches from heat source; broil pork, turning once, until meat is browned on the outside and still slightly pink in the center (internal temperature of tenderloins should be 145°F on meat thermometer), 15 to 20 minutes.

3. To serve, thinly slice pork. Serve on rolls with any juices from broiling pan.

EACH SERVING: About 390 calories (30 percent calories from fat), 32g protein, 35g carbohydrate, 13g total fat (4g saturated), 1g fiber, 70mg cholesterol, 360mg sodium ♥ ♥

Chicken Quesadillas with Avocado Salsa

This tasty Tex-Mex meal calls for lower-fat tortillas and cheese. The splurge: avocado. Though avocados are high in fat, it's mostly the heart-healthy kind; plus, they contain a natural cholesterol reducer.

ACTIVE TIME: 20 minutes
TOTAL TIME: 40 minutes

MAKES: 4 quesadillas

2	teaspoons canola oil
1	green onion, thinly sliced
1	large lime
¼	teaspoon salt
⅛	teaspoon ground black pepper
1	pound skinless, boneless thin-sliced chicken breasts, cut into 1-inch-wide strips
4	burrito-size low-fat flour tortillas
¾	cup (3 ounces) reduced-fat (2%) shredded Mexican cheese blend
½	avocado, peeled, seeded, and cut into ½-inch pieces
¾	cup salsa

1. In nonstick 12-inch skillet, heat oil over medium heat 1 minute. Add green onion and cook about 6 minutes or until tender, stirring occasionally.

2. Meanwhile, from lime, grate 1 teaspoon peel and squeeze 2 tablespoons juice. Evenly season chicken strips on both sides with lime peel, salt, and pepper.

3. Add chicken to green onion in skillet; cook 10 minutes or until chicken is no longer pink inside. Transfer to bowl; stir in lime juice.

4. Evenly divide chicken mixture and cheese on half of each tortilla; fold tortillas over to make 4 quesadillas.

5. In same skillet, cook quesadillas over medium heat, in two batches, 8 minutes per batch or until browned on both sides and heated through. Cut each quesadilla into thirds. Stir avocado into salsa; serve alongside quesadillas.

EACH QUESADILLA: About 400 calories (29 percent calories from fat), 36g protein, 30g carbohydrate, 14g total fat (3g saturated), 10g fiber, 88mg cholesterol, 884mg sodium ♥

Turkey Fajitas

Swapping lean turkey for beef cuts 36 grams of fat, and adding antioxidant-rich sweet peppers boosts heart health. The result: delicioso!

ACTIVE TIME: 25 minutes
TOTAL TIME: 30 minutes

MAKES: 4 main-dish servings

olive oil nonstick cooking spray

2   medium red and/or yellow peppers (4 ounces each), cut into ¼-inch-wide slices

1   medium onion (6 to 8 ounces), cut lengthwise into ¼-inch-wide slices

1   pound turkey-breast cutlets, cut crosswise into ¼-inch-wide strips

3   tablespoons fajita cooking sauce

1   lime

¼   cup reduced-fat sour cream

8   fajita-size flour tortillas (96% fat-free)

1. Spray ridged grill pan with cooking spray; heat over medium-high heat until hot. Spray peppers and onion with cooking spray; place in pan. Cook, tossing often, 12 minutes or until vegetables are tender and grill marks appear.

2. Meanwhile, in bowl, toss turkey strips with cooking sauce; set aside. From lime, grate 1 teaspoon peel. Cut lime into wedges; stir peel into sour cream.

3. Transfer vegetables from grill pan to plate; cover with foil and keep warm.

4. Remove pan from heat; spray with cooking spray. Add turkey and cook over medium-high heat 6 to 7 minutes or until grill marks appear on the outside and turkey is no longer pink inside (cut into turkey to check), turning once. While turkey cooks, wrap tortillas in damp paper towels; microwave on High 1 minute.

5. Top tortillas with turkey and vegetables; fold over. Serve with lime sour cream and lime wedges on the side.

EACH SERVING: About 365 calories (13 percent calories from fat), 33g protein, 44g carbohydrate, 5g total fat (1g saturated), 6g fiber, 82mg cholesterol, 541mg sodium 🟢 🟢

Turkey Burgers with Minted Yogurt Sauce

Pita patties, yogurt, feta, and mint add a taste of Greece to this flavorful but slimmed-down (and heart-healthy) summer favorite.

ACTIVE TIME: 20 minutes
TOTAL TIME: 35 minutes

MAKES: 4 burgers

½   cup plus 2 tablespoons plain fat-free yogurt

2   green onions, green and white parts separated and thinly sliced

½   cup packed fresh mint leaves, finely chopped

1   pound ground turkey breast meat

1½   ounces feta cheese, finely crumbled

1½   teaspoons ground coriander

⅛   teaspoon salt

⅛   teaspoon ground black pepper

2   whole-wheat pitas, cut in half

2   tomatoes, thinly sliced

1. Prepare outdoor grill for covered direct grilling over medium heat.

2. In small bowl, combine ½ cup yogurt, white parts of green onions, and half of chopped mint.

3. In large bowl, with hands, combine turkey, feta, coriander, salt, pepper, green parts of green onions, remaining mint, and remaining yogurt. Mix well, then form into 3 ½-inch round patties each ¾ inch thick.

4. Place turkey patties on hot grill grate; cover and cook 12 to 13 minutes or just until meat loses its pink color throughout, turning once. (Burgers should reach an internal temperature of 165°F.) During last 2 minutes of cooking, add pitas to grill. Cook 2 minutes or until warmed, turning once.

5. Open pitas. Divide burgers, tomato slices, and yogurt sauce among pitas.

EACH BURGER: About 250 calories (16 percent calories from fat), 35g protein, 20g carbohydrate, 5g total fat (2g saturated), 4g fiber, 55mg cholesterol, 412mg sodium ♥

Basic Chicken Burgers

If you're looking for a plain, straightforward burger, here it is. We also have suggestions for jazzing it up, so pick your favorite flavor: teriyaki, barbecue, or herb.

ACTIVE TIME: 20 minutes
TOTAL TIME: 35 minutes

MAKES: 4 burgers

1   pound ground chicken breast
1   medium carrot, peeled and grated (½ cup)
2   green onions, minced
1   garlic clove, crushed with garlic press
4   hamburger buns, split and toasted
sliced cucumber, lettuce leaves, and green onion (optional)

1. Prepare outdoor grill for direct grilling over medium heat.

2. In medium bowl, combine ground chicken, carrot, green onions, and garlic.

3. On waxed paper, shape chicken mixture into four 3 ½-inch round patties (mixture will be very soft and moist).

4. Place patties on hot grill rack over medium heat; if grill has widely spaced grates, place burgers on a perforated grill topper to keep them intact. Grill, turning once, until juices run clear when center of burger is pierced with tip of knife, about 12 minutes. (An instant-read meat thermometer inserted horizontally into center should register 170°F.)

5. Place burgers on toasted buns. Serve with cucumber slices, lettuce leaves, and green onions, if you like.

EACH BURGER: About 275 calories (16 percent calories from fat), 30g protein, 24g carbohydrate, 5g total fat (1g saturated), 2g fiber, 72mg cholesterol, 310mg sodium ♥

TERIYAKI CHICKEN BURGERS: Prepare Basic Burgers as directed, but add *2 tablespoons soy sauce, 1 tablespoon seasoned rice vinegar, 2 teaspoons grated, peeled fresh ginger,* and *2 teaspoons Asian sesame oil* to chicken mixture in step 2. (Ginger will change texture of meat over time; to prevent this, prepare mixture just before grilling.)

EACH TERIYAKI CHICKEN BURGER: About 305 calories (24 percent calories from fat), 31g protein, 26g carbohydrate, 8g total fat (2g saturated), 2g fiber, 72mg cholesterol, 940mg sodium

BARBECUE CHICKEN BURGERS: Prepare Basic Burgers as directed, but add *2 tablespoons chili sauce, 1 tablespoon light (mild) molasses, 2 teaspoons cayenne pepper sauce, 2 teaspoons Worcestershire sauce,* and *1/4 teaspoon salt* to chicken mixture in step 2.

EACH BARBECUE CHICKEN BURGER: About 295 calories (15 percent calories from fat), 31g protein, 30g carbohydrate, 5g total fat (1g saturated), 2g fiber, 72mg cholesterol, 715mg sodium

HERB CHICKEN BURGERS: Prepare Basic Burgers as directed, but add *2 tablespoons finely chopped fresh dill, 1 tablespoon dried mint, 1 tablespoon fresh lemon juice, 1 teaspoon ground cumin, 1/2 teaspoon salt,* and *1/8 teaspoon cayenne (ground red) pepper* to chicken mixture in step 2.

EACH HERB CHICKEN BURGER: About 280 calories (16 percent calories from fat), 31g protein, 25g carbohydrate, 5g total fat (1g saturated), 2g fiber, 72mg cholesterol, 605mg sodium

THE GROUND ROUNDUP

Today's supermarkets offer so many choices in ground meat and poultry. Here's an overview to help you choose.

MEAT	FLAVOR PROFILE	APPROXIMATE NUTRITIONAL VALUES*	COOK-TO-INTERNAL TEMPERATURE
Ground beef, 90% lean	Juicy, rich, bold, robust, hearty	242 calories, 12g fat (5g saturated), 97mg cholesterol	160°F (medium doneness)
Ground lamb	Unique, full flavored, firm texture, aromatic	321 calories, 22g fat (9g saturated), 102mg cholesterol	160°F (medium doneness)
Ground pork	Delicate, mild alternative to beef and poultry	336 calories, 24g fat (9g saturated), 107mg cholesterol	160°F (medium doneness)
Ground chicken	Lean, light texture, tender, subtle flavor	172 calories, 11g fat (3g saturated), 65mg cholesterol	170°F (well-done)
Ground turkey	Moist, delicate flavor, denser texture than chicken	213 calories, 12g fat (3g saturated), 113mg cholesterol	170°F (well-done)

*Per 4-ounce cooked burger. Values vary among brands.

Fish & Shellfish

If you're eating light and healthy, fish and shellfish should make regular appearances on your dinner plate. Seafood is low in fat and a rich source of protein, vitamins, and minerals. And oily fish, such as salmon and tuna, are high in omega-3 fatty acids, which can lower blood cholesterol levels. A couple nights a week, try replacing chicken breasts or red meat with salmon or shrimp, and you and your family will be on your way to a healthier, more varied diet.

If you order fish at restaurants but rarely prepare it at home, let our simple, flavorful recipes lead the way. Keep frozen shrimp in the freezer and you can cook up our shrimp kabobs or a tasty stir-fry in a jiffy. If your kids like tacos, then they'll love our spicy-fish version with avocado and corn.

Dinners like our tuna au poivre and catfish with chipotle salsa can be quickly prepared in a pan, and our Greek-style tilapia and flounder in parchment are roasted in the oven. Our miso-glazed salmon is perfect with fragrant rice, while our pan-seared scallops top a pile of lemony couscous.

Our recipes use readily available options, but if you can't locate the fish or shellfish called for in a recipe, just ask your fishmonger for the best substitution. Many fish can be easily swapped for other varieties with equally good results.

Caramelized Chile Shrimp (recipe page 76)

Mussels with Tomatoes and White Wine

To enjoy every last drop, serve this saucy dish with crusty bread—or a spoon.

ACTIVE TIME: 20 minutes
TOTAL TIME: 45 minutes

MAKES: 8 first-course or 4 main-dish servings

1   tablespoon olive or vegetable oil
1   small onion, chopped
2   garlic cloves, finely chopped
¼   teaspoon crushed red pepper
1   can (14 to 16 ounces) whole tomatoes
¾   cup dry white wine
4   pounds large mussels, scrubbed and debearded (see Tip)
2   tablespoons chopped fresh parsley

1. In nonreactive 5-quart Dutch oven, heat oil over medium heat. Add onion and cook until tender and golden, 6 to 8 minutes. Add garlic and crushed red pepper and cook 30 seconds longer. Stir in tomatoes with their juice and wine, breaking up tomatoes with side of spoon. Heat to boiling; boil 3 minutes.

2. Add mussels; heat to boiling. Reduce heat; cover and simmer until mussels open, about 5 minutes, transferring mussels to large bowl as they open. Discard any mussels that have not opened after 5 minutes. Pour tomato sauce over mussels and sprinkle with parsley.

EACH FIRST-COURSE SERVING: About 105 calories (25 percent calories from fat), 9g protein, 6g carbohydrate, 3g total fat (1g saturated), 1g fiber, 18mg cholesterol, 277mg sodium ♥

TIP: *Scrub mussels well under cold running water. To debeard, grasp the hairlike beard firmly with your thumb and forefinger and pull it away, or scrape it off with a knife. (Cultivated mussels usually do not have beards.)*

MOULES À LA MARINIÈRE: Prepare Mussels with Tomatoes and White Wine as directed, but substitute *butter* for olive oil and *⅓ cup chopped shallots* for onion. Omit crushed red pepper and tomatoes; use *1½ cups dry white wine*.

Crab Boil

A big pot of spiced boiled crabs, a Chesapeake Bay tradition, is a delicious but messy affair. Cover the table with newspaper and have lots of big napkins on hand. Serve with coleslaw and rolls. (If you want to cook crab so you can pick out the meat for use in another recipe, omit the crab boil seasoning and red pepper.)

ACTIVE TIME: 15 minutes
TOTAL TIME: 35 minutes

MAKES: 4 main-dish servings

2	medium onions, coarsely chopped
1	carrot, peeled and coarsely chopped
1	stalk celery, coarsely chopped
1	lemon, sliced
½	cup crab boil seasoning (optional)
1	tablespoon crushed red pepper (optional)
1	tablespoon salt
1	gallon water
1	can (12 ounces) beer
2	dozen live hard-shell blue crabs, rinsed (see Tip)

1. In 12-quart stockpot, combine onions, carrot, celery, lemon, crab boil seasoning and crushed red pepper if using, salt, water, and beer. Heat to boiling over high heat; cook 15 minutes.

2. Using tongs, transfer crabs to stockpot. Cover and heat to boiling; boil 5 minutes (crabs will turn red). With tongs, transfer crabs to colander to drain, then place on warm platter.

3. To eat crab, twist off claws and legs, then crack shell to remove meat. Break off flat pointed apron from underside of crab; remove top shell. Discard feathery gills. With kitchen shears or hands, break body in half down center. With fingers or lobster pick, remove meat.

EACH SERVING: About 150 calories (10 percent calories from fat), 30g protein, 0g carbohydrate, 2g total fat (0g saturated), 0g fiber, 144mg cholesterol, 850mg sodium

TIP: *It's best to cook crabs the day they are purchased, but they can be stored up to two days. Place the crabs in a large shallow bowl, then nestle the bowl in a larger bowl of ice. Cover the crabs with a damp kitchen towel. Refrigerate, replacing the ice as needed.*

Shrimp Kabobs with Asian BBQ Sauce

Fresh ginger and five-spice powder create a delicious sauce for these succulent shrimp kabobs. Serve on a bed of romaine with extra sauce for dipping. For photo, see page 2.

ACTIVE TIME: 15 minutes
TOTAL TIME: 20 minutes
MAKES: 4 main-dish servings

romaine lettuce leaves

1¼ pounds large shrimp, shelled and deveined, with tail part of shell left on, if you like

4 (10- to 12-inch) wooden skewers

⅓ cup hoisin sauce

3 tablespoons ketchup

1½ teaspoons grated, peeled fresh ginger

¼ teaspoon Chinese five-spice powder

2 tablespoons rice vinegar

2 tablespoons water

1. Soak skewers in hot water at least 20 minutes. Lightly grease grill rack. Prepare outdoor grill for direct grilling over medium heat.

2. Arrange romaine on platter and set aside. Thread shrimp on skewers.

3. In small bowl, stir hoisin sauce, ketchup, ginger, five-spice powder, and 1 tablespoon vinegar to make Asian BBQ Sauce. Remove ¼ cup barbecue sauce to ramekin; stir in water and remaining 1 tablespoon vinegar and reserve to use as dipping sauce.

4. Brush shrimp with some barbecue sauce from bowl. Place shrimp on hot grill rack over medium heat and cook 2 minutes. Brush with more sauce; turn, brush with remaining sauce, and grill until shrimp turn opaque throughout, 1 to 2 minutes longer.

5. Serve shrimp on skewers over romaine with reserved dipping sauce.

EACH SERVING: About 185 calories (14 percent calories from fat), 25g protein, 13g carbohydrate, 3g total fat (1g saturated), 1g fiber, 175mg cholesterol, 540mg sodium ◔

Shrimp and Asparagus Stir-Fry

Flavored with ginger, soy, and sesame, this entreé is rich in vitamins and minerals (thanks to brown rice and asparagus).

ACTIVE TIME: 15 minutes
TOTAL TIME: 30 minutes

MAKES: 4 main-dish servings

1   cup quick-cooking (10-minute) brown rice

3   teaspoons Asian sesame oil

1½ pounds asparagus, trimmed and cut into
     1-inch pieces

1   pound medium shrimp, shelled and deveined

1   tablespoon grated, peeled fresh ginger

2   tablespoons reduced-sodium soy sauce

2   tablespoons fresh lime juice

¼   cup loosely packed fresh basil leaves,
     thinly sliced

1. Cook rice as label directs.

2. Meanwhile, in nonstick 12-inch skillet, heat 2 teaspoons sesame oil over medium heat 1 minute. Add asparagus and cook 7 to 8 minutes or until asparagus is tender-crisp, stirring occasionally. Add shrimp and ginger; cook 5 to 6 minutes or until shrimp are opaque throughout, stirring occasionally.

3. Stir in soy sauce, lime juice, basil, and remaining 1 teaspoon sesame oil; remove from heat. Serve over rice.

EACH SERVING: About 265 calories (24 percent calories from fat), 29g protein, 22g carbohydrate, 7g total fat (1g saturated), 2g fiber, 172mg cholesterol, 455mg sodium

FROZEN SHRIMP TO THE RESCUE

Shrimp, with just fewer than 2 grams of fat in a 4-ounce serving, should be a savvy dieter's go-to seafood. Although fresh shrimp can be expensive, frozen shrimp, available at wholesale food clubs and larger supermarkets, is a bargain. Because it is flash-frozen for easy transport, the flavor and texture are preserved. Keep some on hand in the freezer and it will be a snap to whip up low-fat stir-fries, pastas, and main-dish salads. The shrimp is sold individually frozen in bags or in a block. To defrost, put the individually frozen shrimp in a colander and place under cold running water until thawed. For block-frozen shrimp, place under cold running water and pull off the amount of shrimp you need as they thaw; return the remaining block of shrimp to the freezer immediately.

Caramelized Chile Shrimp

Thanks to a trio of insta-ingredients—preshelled shrimp, thin vermicelli, and bagged broccoli—this streamlined seafood stir-fry is ideal on time-is-tight nights. For photo, see page 70.

ACTIVE TIME: 15 minutes
TOTAL TIME: 25 minutes
MAKES: 4 main-dish servings

6	ounces rice stick noodles (rice vermicelli)
1	pound broccoli florets
1	green onion, finely chopped
¼	teaspoon salt
3	tablespoons sugar
1	tablespoon water
1	tablespoon vegetable oil
3	garlic cloves, very thinly sliced
¼	teaspoon crushed red pepper
1	tablespoon reduced-sodium Asian fish sauce
1	pound jumbo shrimp, shelled and deveined
¼	cup packed fresh cilantro leaves
¼	teaspoon ground black pepper

1. In heavy 12-inch skillet, heat *1 inch water* to boiling over high heat. Add noodles and cook 1 to 2 minutes or until just tender. With tongs, transfer noodles to fine-mesh sieve. Rinse under cold water and drain.

2. When water in skillet returns to boiling, add broccoli. Cook 3 minutes or until tender-crisp; drain and transfer to large bowl. Toss with green onion and salt. Wipe skillet dry.

3. In same skillet, cook sugar and water over medium-high (stirring just until sugar dissolves), 3 to 4 minutes or until mixture turns dark amber. Stir in oil, garlic, and red pepper. Cook 10 seconds, then stir in fish sauce and shrimp.

4. Cook 2 to 3 minutes or until shrimp just turn opaque throughout, stirring frequently. Remove from heat, and stir in cilantro and black pepper.

5. Evenly divide noodles and broccoli among four dinner plates. Spoon shrimp with chile sauce on top of noodles.

EACH SERVING: About 340 calories (13 percent calories from fat), 22g protein, 53g carbohydrate, 5g total fat (1g saturated), 4g fiber, 168mg cholesterol, 600mg sodium ◐

Pan-Seared Scallops with Lemon Couscous

Lemony couscous and peppery arugula create a flavorful bed for these succulent scallops.

ACTIVE TIME: 20 minutes
TOTAL TIME: 45 minutes

MAKES: 6 main-dish servings

1	large red pepper
1	onion
12	ounces medium mushrooms
1	pound sea scallops
4	teaspoons olive oil or vegetable oil
1	lemon
1½	cups water
1	cup couscous (Moroccan pasta)
¾	teaspoon salt
1	package (8 ounces) frozen sugar snap peas
2	tablespoons soy sauce
2	bunches arugula (8 ounces) stems trimmed

1. Thinly slice red pepper and onion. Cut each mushroom into quarters. Rinse scallops under cold running water to remove sand from crevices. Pat scallops dry with paper towels.

2. In nonstick 12-inch skillet over medium-high heat, heat 2 teaspoons oil and cook red pepper and onion until golden brown. Remove mixture to plate.

3. In same skillet, heat 1 teaspoon oil; cook mushrooms until golden brown. Remove mushrooms to plate with red-pepper mixture.

4. Meanwhile, from lemon, grate ½ teaspoon peel and squeeze 1½ teaspoons juice. In 2-quart saucepan over high heat, heat lemon juice and water to boiling. Stir in couscous and salt. Cover saucepan and remove from heat. Let stand 5 minutes; stir in lemon peel. Keep warm.

5. Prepare frozen sugar snap peas as label directs; drain.

6. In same skillet over medium-high heat, heat remaining 1 teaspoon oil and cook scallops until opaque throughout, stirring occasionally, 3 to 4 minutes. Return vegetable mixture to skillet with scallops; stir in soy sauce. Cook mixture over medium-high heat until heated through; stir in snap peas.

7. Arrange arugula on plates. Top with couscous and scallop mixture.

EACH SERVING: About 265 calories (14 percent calories from fat), 20g protein, 36g carbohydrate, 4g total fat (1g saturated), 12g fiber, 25mg cholesterol, 770mg sodium ♥

Grilled Fish Tacos

Coated with a bold, Baja-style rub of cayenne and oregano and then char-crusted on the grill, the tilapia in these taqueria-worthy tacos tastes anything but fishy. A from-scratch salsa with corn and avocado adds to the meal's authenticity.

ACTIVE TIME: 15 minutes
TOTAL TIME: 20 minutes
MAKES: 4 main-dish servings

1	large lemon
2½	teaspoon vegetable oil
½	teaspoon plus pinch salt
2	ears corn, husked
1	avocado, cut in half and pitted
3	garlic cloves, crushed with press
½	teaspoon dried oregano
¼	teaspoon cayenne (ground red) pepper
1	pound skinless tilapia fillets (see Tip)
12	corn tortillas
1	large ripe tomato, finely chopped

fresh cilantro leaves and lime wedges, for serving

1. Prepare outdoor grill for direct grilling over medium-high heat. From lemon, grate 2 teaspoons peel and squeeze 2 tablespoons juice.

2. Use ½ teaspoon oil and pinch salt to rub all over corn and cut sides of avocado; set aside on a plate. On another plate, combine garlic, oregano, cayenne, lemon peel, ¼ teaspoon salt, and remaining 2 teaspoons oil. Place fish on mixture and rub all over to coat.

3. Place fish, corn, and avocado, cut sides down, on hot grill grate. Cook fish 3 to 4 minutes or until opaque throughout, turning over once; cook vegetables 5 minutes or until charred, turning occasionally.

4. Transfer fish, corn, and avocado to cutting board. Let cool while warming tortillas: Place tortillas on grill in single layer and cook 1 minute, turning once. Stack on large sheet of foil and wrap tightly.

5. Cut kernels from corncobs. Peel and finely chop avocado. Break fish into large chunks. In large bowl, mix together tomato, corn, avocado, lemon juice, and remaining ¼ teaspoon salt. Divide fish and tomato mixture among tortillas and serve with cilantro and lime wedges.

EACH SERVING: About 420 calories (28 percent calories from fat), 31g protein, 49g carbohydrate, 13g total fat (2g saturated), 9g fiber, 52mg cholesterol, 425mg sodium ♥ ♥ ⓥ

TIP: *Flounder, catfish, or any mild white fish would be a good substitute for the tilapia. Grill fish fillets only 8 to 10 minutes per inch of thickness.*

Greek-Style Tilapia

This healthy Mediterranean fish dish is ready in 30 minutes.

ACTIVE TIME: 20 minutes
TOTAL TIME: 30 minutes
MAKES: 4 main-dish servings

2	lemons
1½	pounds tilapia fillets
1	tablespoon fresh oregano leaves, chopped, plus sprigs for garnish
¼	teaspoon salt
¼	teaspoon ground black pepper
1	pint grape tomatoes, cut lengthwise in half
8	ounces orzo

1. Preheat oven to 400°F. From lemons, grate ½ teaspoon peel and squeeze ¼ cup juice.

2. In 13" by 9" glass or ceramic baking dish, arrange tilapia fillets. Evenly sprinkle fillets with lemon juice and peel, chopped oregano, salt, and pepper. Add tomatoes to baking dish around tilapia; cover with foil and roast 16 to 18 minutes or until tilapia is opaque throughout and tomatoes are tender.

3. Meanwhile, heat covered 4-quart saucepan of salted *water* to boiling over high heat. Add orzo and cook as label directs. Drain well.

4. Serve tilapia, tomatoes, and orzo with juices from baking dish.

EACH SERVING: About 395 calories (14 percent calories from fat), 36g protein, 50g carbohydrate, 6g total fat (0g saturated), 2g fiber, 0mg cholesterol, 310mg sodium ♥ ♥

Catfish with Chipotle Salsa over Polenta

Polenta, the Italian cousin of Southern grits, is made from finely ground yellow cornmeal. We make this side dish with 1 percent milk and chicken broth to keep it low in fat.

ACTIVE TIME: 30 minutes
TOTAL TIME: 50 minutes
MAKES: 4 main-dish servings

4	large plum tomatoes (about 1 pound), each cut lengthwise in half
1	small red onion, cut crosswise into ½-inch-thick rings
	nonstick cooking spray
4	catfish fillets (about 6 ounces each)
¾	teaspoon chipotle chile powder
¾	teaspoon salt
2	cups low-fat (1%) milk
1	can (14 to 14½ ounces) reduced-sodium chicken broth (1¾ cups)
1	cup water
¾	cup instant polenta
1	cup fresh corn kernels (from 2 ears corn) or 1 cup frozen (thawed) corn kernels
2	teaspoons fresh lime juice

1. Preheat large ridged grill pan over medium-high heat. On sheet of waxed paper, place tomato halves and onion slices. Spray vegetables on both sides with nonstick cooking spray. Place tomatoes and onion on grill pan and cook 10 minutes or until lightly browned and softened, turning over once. Transfer vegetables to cutting board.

2. While tomatoes and onion are cooking, place catfish fillets on same waxed paper. Sprinkle with ½ teaspoon chipotle chile powder and ¼ teaspoon salt to season both sides, then spray both sides with nonstick cooking spray.

3. Place catfish on grill pan over medium-high heat; cook 7 to 8 minutes or just until it turns opaque throughout, turning over once.

4. While catfish is cooking, prepare polenta: In 3-quart saucepan, combine milk, broth, water, and ¼ teaspoon salt; cover and heat to boiling over high heat. Remove cover; slowly whisk in polenta and cook until mixture begins to thicken, stirring constantly. Reduce heat to low; cover saucepan and simmer 5 minutes, stirring occasionally. Stir in corn. Remove saucepan from heat.

5. Coarsely chop grilled tomatoes and onion; transfer, with any juices, to medium bowl. Stir in lime juice and remaining ¼ teaspoon each chipotle chile powder and salt. Makes about 1¾ cups salsa.

6. To serve, divide polenta among four dinner plates; top with grilled catfish and tomato-chipotle salsa.

EACH SERVING: About 410 calories (26 percent calories from fat), 32g protein, 43g carbohydrate, 12g total fat (3g saturated), 3g fiber, 90mg cholesterol, 870mg sodium

Asian-Style Flounder Baked in Parchment

Baking in parchment packets is a simple nonfat way to seal in the juices and flavor of delicate fish. You may substitute aluminum foil for the parchment paper.

TOTAL TIME: 25 minutes
MAKES: 4 main-dish servings

2	large green onions
2	tablespoons soy sauce
2	tablespoons seasoned rice vinegar
4	flounder fillets (6 ounces each)
4	sheets cooking parchment or foil (12" by 16" each, folded in half to 12" by 8")
2	teaspoons grated, peeled fresh ginger

1. Preheat oven to 425°F. Cut green onion tops into 2-inch by ¼-inch strips; reserve for garnish. Thinly slice white part of green onions.

2. In cup, combine soy sauce and vinegar.

3. Place 1 flounder fillet on one side of each opened parchment sheet. Sprinkle with ginger and sliced green onions; drizzle with soy mixture. Fold parchment over fish; beginning at a corner where parchment is folded, make ½-inch-wide folds, overlapping previous folds, until packet is completely sealed. Packet will resemble half circle. Place packets in jelly-roll pan. Bake 8 minutes (packets will puff up and brown).

4. To serve, cut packets open and garnish fish with reserved green-onion strips.

EACH SERVING: About 170 calories (11 percent calories from fat), 33g protein, 3g carbohydrate, 2g total fat (0g saturated), 0g fiber, 82mg cholesterol, 802mg sodium ●

Pasta with Tuna Puttanesca

We've used tuna instead of anchovies in this tasty no-cook twist on traditional puttanesca sauce. For best flavor use extra-virgin olive oil.

ACTIVE TIME: 5 minutes
TOTAL TIME: 15 minutes
MAKES: 6 main-dish servings

1	package (16 ounces) fusilli or corkscrew pasta
3	tablespoons capers, drained and chopped
3	tablespoons minced shallot
2	tablespoons red wine vinegar
1	tablespoon olive oil
½	teaspoon grated lemon peel
½	teaspoon salt
¼	teaspoon coarsely ground black pepper
1	can (6 ounces) light tuna in olive oil
2	medium bunches watercress, tough stems removed
½	cup loosely packed fresh basil leaves, chopped

1. In large saucepot, cook pasta as label directs.

2. Meanwhile, in a large bowl, with fork, stir capers, shallot, vinegar, oil, lemon peel, salt, and pepper until well mixed. Add undrained tuna and watercress; toss well.

3. When pasta has reached desired doneness, remove ½ *cup pasta cooking water*. Drain pasta and return to saucepot. Add tuna mixture, reserved cooking water, and basil; toss well.

EACH SERVING: About 375 calories (19 percent calories from fat), 17g protein, 58g carbohydrate, 8g total fat (1g saturated), 3g fiber, 4mg cholesterol, 540mg sodium ●

Tuna au Poivre with Lemon-Caper Lentils

Lean tuna replaces fattier beef loin steak in this favorite—and a surprise side of lentils, in place of the expected calorie-laden French fries, adds an earthy boost of fiber.

ACTIVE TIME: 10 minutes
TOTAL TIME: 35 minutes
MAKES: 4 main-dish servings

2 ²/₃ cups water

1 ¹/₃ cups green lentils

1 teaspoon salt

4 tuna steaks, 1 inch thick (6 ounces each)

4 teaspoons cracked black peppercorns

1 tablespoon olive oil

1 medium shallot, finely chopped

1 cup reduced-sodium chicken broth

1 tablespoon capers, chopped

1 tablespoon fresh lemon juice

1. In 2-quart saucepan, combine water, lentils, and ¹/₂ teaspoon salt; heat to boiling over high heat. Reduce heat to low; cover and simmer 20 to 25 minutes or until lentils are tender. Drain lentils and return to pan; cover to keep warm.

2. Meanwhile, evenly season tuna, on both sides, with remaining ¹/₂ teaspoon salt and all pepper, pressing in pepper. In 12-inch cast-iron skillet, heat oil over medium-high heat until hot. Add tuna and cook 5 to 8 minutes for medium or until desired doneness, turning over once. Transfer to plate; cover to keep warm.

3. To same skillet, add shallot and cook 1 minute, stirring. Add broth and capers; heat to boiling. Boil 3 minutes or until liquid is reduced by half. Add lentils; heat through. Remove from heat; stir in lemon juice. Serve tuna over lentils.

EACH SERVING: About 445 calories (12 percent calories from fat), 58g protein, 40g carbohydrate, 6g total fat (1g saturated), 20g fiber, 76mg cholesterol, 830mg sodium 🌱

Fish & Shellfish **83**

Miso-Glazed Salmon

For a satisfying low-fat dinner, we spread a sweet and savory sauce on salmon fillets and broil them to make a rich glaze. Serve with a side of aromatic jasmine or basmati rice, or a salad of edamame and sliced radishes.

ACTIVE TIME: 10 minutes
TOTAL TIME: 20 minutes
MAKES: 4 main-dish servings

¼	cup white miso (see Tip)
5	teaspoons sugar
4	teaspoons seasoned rice vinegar
1	tablespoon water
1	tablespoon minced, peeled fresh ginger
4	salmon fillets, 1 inch thick (5 ounces each)
1	green onion, thinly sliced diagonally

1. Preheat broiler. Lightly spray rack in broiling pan with nonstick cooking spray.

2. In small bowl, mix miso, sugar, vinegar, water, and ginger; set aside.

3. Place salmon fillets on rack in broiling pan. Place pan in broiler at closest position to heat source; broil salmon 5 minutes. Remove pan from broiler and spread half of miso mixture on salmon; broil 1 minute longer.

4. Remove pan from broiler; turn salmon over and top with remaining miso mixture. Broil salmon until miso mixture is bubbly and salmon is opaque throughout, 3 to 4 minutes longer. Sprinkle with green onion before serving.

EACH SERVING: About 260 calories (24 percent calories from fat), 35g protein, 13g carbohydrate, 7g total fat (1g saturated), 0g fiber, 86mg cholesterol, 870mg sodium ●

TIP: *Miso—a paste made of fermented soybeans—comes in a variety of flavors, colors, and textures that fall into three basic categories: red, which has a strong flavor; golden, which is mild; and white, which is mellow and slightly sweet. Miso can be purchased in health-food stores and Asian markets.*

Mustard-Dill Salmon with Herbed Potatoes

A light and creamy sauce adds piquant flavor to succulent salmon. After you make the sauce, sauté snow peas in a nonstick skillet with a teaspoon of vegetable oil for a healthy side dish.

ACTIVE TIME: 20 minutes
TOTAL TIME: 30 minutes

MAKES: 4 main-dish servings

12   ounces small red potatoes, cut into 1-inch chunks

12   ounces small white potatoes, cut into 1-inch chunks

1½   teaspoons salt

3   tablespoons chopped fresh dill

½   teaspoon coarsely ground black pepper

4   pieces salmon fillet (6 ounces each)

2   tablespoons light mayonnaise

1   tablespoon white wine vinegar

2   teaspoons Dijon mustard

¾   teaspoon sugar

1. In a 3-quart saucepan, heat potatoes, 1 teaspoon salt, and enough *water* to cover to boiling over high heat. Reduce heat to low; cover and simmer until potatoes are fork-tender, about 15 minutes. Drain potatoes and toss with 1 tablespoon dill, ¼ teaspoon salt, and ¼ teaspoon pepper; keep the potatoes warm.

2. Meanwhile, preheat boiler. Grease rack in broiling pan. Place salmon on rack; sprinkle with ⅛ teaspoon salt and ⅛ teaspoon pepper. Place broiling pan at closest position to heat source. Broil until salmon is just opaque throughout, 8 to 10 minutes.

3. While salmon is broiling, prepare sauce: In small bowl, mix mayonnaise, vinegar, mustard, sugar, remaining 2 tablespoons dill, ⅛ teaspoon salt, and ⅛ teaspoon pepper.

4. Serve salmon with sauce and potatoes.

EACH SERVING: About 335 calories (19 percent calories from fat), 37g protein, 31g carbohydrate, 7g total fat (1g saturated), 2g fiber, 86mg cholesterol, 655mg sodium

GET YOUR OMEGA-3s

Despite a reputation for clogging arteries and packing on unwanted pounds, all fats are not villainous. Indeed, one type of polyunsaturated fat, omega-3, is thought to combat heart disease. Omega-3s help inhibit the formation of blood clots and reduce the incidence of heartbeat abnormalities. You'll find omega-3s in fish—and the oilier the fish, the more omega-3 it contains. So, be sure to include oily fish like salmon, bluefin tuna, mackerel, and sardines in your diet once a week.

4

Chicken & Turkey

On busy weeknights or when unexpected company drops in for dinner, poultry is the solution many of us turn to again and again—and with good reason. It's simple to prepare in a multitude of satisfying ways, whether you quickly stir-fry, pan-fry, or grill it, or stick it in the oven to slowly braise in its own juices or roast until it's succulent and golden brown. Better still, it's a lean and healthy option, especially if you prepare white meat or remove the skin from dark meat before serving (see "The Skinny on Poultry," page 96).

In this chapter, we offer a selection of our favorite go-to recipes, beginning with a bevy of skillet dishes paired with flavorful sauces you can whip up in the same pan—just the thing when you need to get dinner on the table in 30 minutes or less. Our apple-dijon chicken is speedy to prepare, but perfect for special nights when you want to cook to impress.

Then it's onto the stir-fries, from a zesty tangerine chicken tossed with broccoli flowerets and carrots to a Thai-inspired dish with coconut milk. If grilling is your quick-cooking method of choice, then our poultry recipes paired with three different fruity salsas are sure to inspire you.

But if you prefer to spend a little time upfront, and then let the oven do its magic, you'll welcome our recipes for roasted birds, baked "fried" chicken, and even a (turkey) shepherd's pie.

Tangerine Chicken Stir-Fry (recipe page 90)

Apple-Dijon Chicken

*The maple syrup in this autumn-inspired dish
enhances the flavor of the apples and provides a
sweet counterpoint to the zesty Dijon mustard.
For best results, look for 100 percent pure maple
syrup, not "maple-flavored" syrup, which is a
mixture of corn syrup and a very small amount
of real maple syrup or extract.*

ACTIVE TIME: 15 minutes
TOTAL TIME: 30 minutes

MAKES: 4 main-dish servings

4   medium skinless, boneless chicken breast
     halves (1¼ pounds)

½   teaspoon salt

⅛   teaspoon freshly ground black pepper

1   tablespoon olive oil

2   Golden Delicious apples, each cored and
     cut crosswise into 6 rings

1   small red onion, sliced

¾   cup reduced-sodium chicken broth

2   tablespoons maple syrup

1   tablespoon Dijon mustard with seeds

⅓   cup half-and-half

1   teaspoon cornstarch

1. With meat mallet or bottom of skillet, pound
chicken breast halves (placed between two
sheets plastic wrap) to even ½-inch thickness;
sprinkle with ¼ teaspoon salt and pepper.

2. In nonstick 12-inch skillet, heat oil over
medium heat until hot. Add chicken breasts and
cook, turning once, until chicken is browned on
both sides and loses its pink color throughout, 6
to 7 minutes. Transfer chicken breasts to platter; cover loosely with foil to keep warm. Do not
wash skillet.

3. Meanwhile, in microwave-safe pie plate,
combine apples and onion. Cover with waxed
paper and microwave on High, stirring once,
until tender, 3 to 4 minutes.

4. Add apple mixture to skillet and cook over
medium heat until browned, about 2 minutes.
Add broth, maple syrup, mustard, and remaining ¼ teaspoon salt. Cook until broth mixture is
slightly reduced, about 2 minutes.

5. In small bowl, blend half-and-half and cornstarch until smooth; stir into apple mixture with
juices from platter. Cook until sauce is slightly
thickened, about 1 minute. To serve, spoon sauce
over chicken.

EACH SERVING: About 295 calories (24 percent
calories from fat), 34g protein, 21g carbohydrate, 8g
total fat (2g saturated), 2g fiber, 90mg cholesterol,
500mg sodium ⊙

Basil-Orange Chicken with Couscous

Marinating the chicken in orange and basil gives it a bright, fresh flavor. Served over whole-wheat couscous with steamed sugar snap peas, this light dish is perfect for warmer weather. For photo, see page 5.

ACTIVE TIME: 20 minutes
TOTAL TIME: 30 minutes

MAKES: 4 main-dish servings

2	large navel oranges
3	lemons
1/2	cup packed fresh basil leaves, chopped
2	tablespoons olive oil
3/8	teaspoon salt
3/8	teaspoon ground black pepper
4	medium skinless, boneless chicken breast halves (1 1/2 pounds)
1/2	teaspoon sugar
1	cup whole-wheat couscous
1	package (8 ounces) stringless sugar snap peas

1. From 1 orange, grate 1 1/2 teaspoons peel and squeeze 4 tablespoons juice. From 2 lemons, grate 1 1/2 teaspoons peel and squeeze 1/3 cup juice. Cut remaining orange and lemon into slices and set aside.

2. In medium bowl, combine 1 teaspoon of each peel and 1 tablespoon orange juice with half of basil, 1 tablespoon olive oil, 1/4 teaspoon salt, and 1/4 teaspoon pepper.

3. Place chicken breast between two sheets plastic wrap and, with flat side of meat mallet, pound to an even 1/2-inch thickness. Add chicken to citrus mixture, turning to coat; set aside.

4. In small pitcher or bowl, combine sugar, remaining 1/8 teaspoon salt, remaining 1/8 teaspoon pepper, citrus peels, citrus juices, basil, and oil; set aside. (Dish can be made to this point up to 8 hours ahead. Cover chicken and citrus sauce and refrigerate.)

5. Preheat large ridged grill pan or prepare outdoor grill for direct grilling over medium-high heat. Meanwhile, prepare couscous as label directs. In 4-quart saucepan filled with *1/2 inch water*, place a vegetable steamer. Heat to boiling over high.

6. Add chicken to hot grill pan or grate; cook 4 minutes. Turn chicken over and cook 3 to 4 minutes longer or until no longer pink in center. Grill reserved citrus slices as well.

7. While chicken is cooking on second side, add snap peas to steamer; cook 2 to 3 minutes or until tender-crisp. Fluff couscous and spoon onto large platter; top with chicken and snap peas. Drizzle sauce over all. Garnish with grilled citrus slices.

EACH SERVING: About 400 calories (20 percent calories from fat), 46g protein, 33g carbohydrate, 9g total fat (1g saturated), 6g fiber, 99mg cholesterol, 365mg sodium ♥ ♥ ⓥ 🍲

Tangerine Chicken Stir-Fry

Toss stir-fried chicken and mixed vegetables with a citrus-infused sauce for a quick and delicious meal. For photo, see page 86.

ACTIVE TIME: 20 minutes
TOTAL TIME: 30 minutes
MAKES: 4 main-dish servings

3   tangerines
¼   cup dry sherry
1   tablespoon grated, peeled fresh ginger
1   teaspoon Asian sesame oil
1   teaspoon plus 1 tablespoon cornstarch
2   tablespoons reduced-sodium soy sauce
1½   pounds skinless, boneless chicken breast halves, cut into ½-inch-wide strips
1   cup quick-cooking (10-minute) brown rice
4   teaspoons vegetable oil
1   bag (12 ounces) broccoli florets
2   carrots, peeled and thinly sliced diagonally
3   green onions, cut into 1-inch pieces
⅓   cup water

1. From 1 tangerine, with vegetable peeler, remove peel in strips. Using small knife, remove and discard any white pith from peel; set peel aside. Into 1-cup liquid measuring cup, squeeze ½ cup juice from tangerines. Stir in sherry, ginger, sesame oil, and 1 teaspoon cornstarch; set juice mixture aside.

2. In medium bowl, combine soy sauce and remaining 1 tablespoon cornstarch. Add chicken and toss to coat; set chicken mixture aside.

3. Cook rice as label directs. Meanwhile, in 12-inch skillet, heat 2 teaspoons vegetable oil over medium-high until hot. Add peel and cook 1 minute or until lightly browned. With tongs or slotted spoon, transfer peel to large bowl.

4. To same skillet, add broccoli, carrots, and green onions; stir to coat with oil. Add water; cover and cook 4 minutes, stirring once. Uncover and cook 1 minute longer or until vegetables are tender-crisp, stirring frequently (stir-frying). Transfer vegetables to bowl with peel.

5. To same skillet, add remaining 2 teaspoons vegetable oil; reduce heat to medium. Add chicken mixture and cook 6 to 7 minutes or until chicken is golden and loses its pink color throughout, stirring frequently. Transfer chicken to bowl with cooked vegetables.

6. Add juice mixture to skillet and heat to boiling over medium-high heat; boil 1 minute, stirring until browned bits are loosened. Return chicken and vegetables to skillet and cook 1 minute to heat through, stirring. To serve, spoon brown rice into four shallow dinner bowls; top with chicken and vegetables.

EACH SERVING: About 390 calories (21 percent calories from fat), 45g protein, 32g carbohydrate, 9g total fat (1g saturated), 5g fiber, 99mg cholesterol, 420mg sodium ♥ ♥ ⊗

Thai-Style Coconut Chicken

Unsweetened coconut milk, a staple in Thai cuisine readily available at the supermarket, is a great ingredient to have handy if you're looking for rich-tasting, long-simmering flavor but are pressed for time. If you can't find jasmine rice, substitute basmati or Texmati, which is a cross between American long-grain rice and basmati.

ACTIVE TIME: 20 minutes
TOTAL TIME: 30 minutes

MAKES: 4 main-dish servings

1	cup jasmine rice or long-grain white rice
1	can (14 ounces) light coconut milk (not cream of coconut)
1	cup canned or homemade chicken broth (page 57)
1	tablespoon cornstarch
4	thin slices peeled fresh ginger
2	strips (3" by ½") fresh lime peel
1	pound skinless, boneless chicken breasts, cut into ½-inch-wide strips
6	ounces snow peas (2 cups), strings removed
1	tablespoon reduced-sodium Asian fish sauce
¼	cup loosely packed fresh cilantro leaves, chopped
lime wedges	

1. Prepare rice as label directs.

2. Meanwhile, in 12-inch nonstick skillet, stir coconut milk, broth, cornstarch, ginger, and lime peel; heat to boiling over medium-high heat, stirring frequently. Boil 1 minute.

3. Add chicken and snow peas to skillet; cover and cook until chicken loses its pink color throughout, 4 to 5 minutes. Remove skillet from heat; stir in fish sauce and cilantro. Serve with rice and lime wedges.

EACH SERVING: About 405 calories (17 percent calories from fat), 31g protein, 43g carbohydrate, 11g total (6g saturated), 2g fiber, 66mg cholesterol, 465mg sodium ❤

Coffee-Spice Chicken and Fruit-Basil Salsa

A jerk-style seasoning of Jamaican allspice and java gives this Caribbean chicken its caffeinated kick. Balancing the heat: a cooling summer salsa of just-picked nectarines and juicy watermelon.

ACTIVE TIME: 30 minutes
TOTAL TIME: 40 minutes

MAKES: 8 main-dish servings

3	cups seedless watermelon cubes, cut into ½-inch chunks (from 4-pound piece of watermelon)
1	large ripe nectarine, pitted and cut into ½-inch chunks
3	tablespoons finely chopped red onion
1	tablespoon fresh lemon juice
2	tablespoons instant coffee
1	tablespoon grated, peeled fresh ginger
1	tablespoon olive oil
1¼	teaspoons ground allspice
¾	teaspoon salt
8	skinless, boneless chicken breast halves (3 pounds)
½	cup packed fresh basil leaves, coarsely chopped

1. In medium bowl, combine watermelon, nectarine, red onion, and lemon juice. Cover and refrigerate while preparing chicken. Makes about 4 cups salsa.

2. Prepare outdoor grill for covered direct grilling over medium heat.

3. In large bowl, with spoon or fingers, press coffee to pulverize. Add ginger, oil, allspice, and ½ teaspoon salt; stir to combine. Add chicken and toss to evenly coat with spice mixture (you may need to pat spice mixture onto chicken with fingers).

4. Place chicken breasts on hot grill rack. Cover and cook 8 to 10 minutes or until juices run clear when thickest part of chicken is pierced with tip of knife, turning once. Transfer chicken to cutting board and let rest 5 minutes. Meanwhile, stir basil and remaining ¼ teaspoon salt into salsa. Slice chicken crosswise and serve with salsa on the side.

EACH SERVING: About 235 calories (15 percent calories from fat), 40g protein, 8g carbohydrate, 4g total fat (1g saturated), 1g fiber, 99mg cholesterol, 310mg sodium ♥

Lemon-Oregano Chicken

This fresh-flavored chicken dish is perfect for outdoor grilling on one of those surprisingly warm days in early spring. For even cooking, it's a good idea to pound chicken breasts to a uniform thickness with a meat mallet.

ACTIVE TIME: 15 minutes
TOTAL TIME: 30 minutes
MAKES: 4 main-dish servings

3	medium zucchini (8 ounces each)
2	tablespoons olive oil
½	teaspoon salt
½	cup loosely packed fresh mint leaves, chopped
4	medium skinless, boneless chicken breast halves (1½ pounds)
3	lemons
1	tablespoon chopped fresh oregano
½	teaspoon coarsely ground black pepper

1. Prepare outdoor grill for covered direct grilling over medium heat.

2. With mandoline or sharp knife, slice zucchini very thinly lengthwise. In large bowl, toss zucchini with 1 tablespoon oil, ¼ teaspoon salt, and half of mint.

3. Place chicken breast between two sheets plastic wrap and, with meat mallet, pound to uniform ¼-inch thickness. From 2 lemons, grate 1 tablespoon peel and squeeze 2 tablespoons juice. Cut remaining lemon into 4 wedges; set aside. In medium bowl, combine lemon peel and juice with oregano, pepper, and remaining 1 tablespoon oil and ¼ teaspoon salt. Add chicken to bowl and toss until evenly coated.

4. Place zucchini slices, in batches, on hot grill rack over medium heat and cook until grill marks appear and zucchini is tender, 2 to 4 minutes, turning over once. Remove zucchini from grill; place on large platter and sprinkle with remaining mint.

5. Place chicken on hot grill rack. Cover grill and cook chicken until juices run clear when chicken is pierced with tip of knife, 6 to 8 minutes, turning over once. Transfer chicken to platter with zucchini; serve with lemon wedges.

EACH SERVING: About 280 calories (29 percent calories from fat), 42g protein, 8g carbohydrate, 9g total fat (2g saturated), 3g fiber, 99mg cholesterol, 390mg sodium ♥ ♥

Prosciutto Turkey Cutlets with Melon

When buying turkey cutlets for this recipe, make sure not to get ones that are very thinly sliced for scaloppine.

ACTIVE TIME: 20 minutes
TOTAL TIME: 30 minutes

MAKES: 4 servings

2   limes

1½ cups chopped, peeled cantaloupe

1½ cups chopped, peeled honeydew melon

1   small Kirby cucumber, shredded (½ cup)

1   jalapeño chile, seeded and finely chopped

¼   cup loosely packed fresh basil leaves, chopped

¼   teaspoon salt

4   turkey breast cutlets (1 pound total)

¼   teaspoon coarsely ground black pepper

4   ounces thinly sliced prosciutto

1. Grease grill rack. Prepare outdoor grill for direct grilling over medium heat.

2. From 1 lime, grate 1 teaspoon peel and squeeze 2 tablespoons juice. Cut remaining lime into 4 wedges and set aside. In bowl, combine lime juice, cantaloupe, melon, cucumber, jalapeño, basil, and salt. Makes about 3 cups salsa.

3. Sprinkle turkey cutlets with lime peel and pepper. Wrap turkey cutlets with prosciutto, pressing prosciutto firmly onto turkey.

4. Place turkey on hot grill rack over medium heat and cook until turkey loses its pink color throughout, 5 to 7 minutes, turning over once. Transfer turkey to plate; serve with salsa and lime wedges.

EACH SERVING TURKEY: About 185 calories (20 percent calories from fat), 35g protein, 0g carbohydrate, 4g total fat (1g saturated), 0g fiber, 86mg cholesterol, 815mg sodium ♥

EACH ¼ CUP SALSA: About 10 calories (0 calories from fat), 0g protein, 3g carbohydrate, 0g total fat, 0g fiber, 0mg cholesterol, 50mg sodium ♥ ♥

Honey-Mustard Chicken and Potatoes

Everything for this meal cooks in the oven at the same time. If you'd like to add something green, steamed fresh green beans make a delicious accompaniment.

ACTIVE TIME: 10 minutes
TOTAL TIME: 1 hour 35 minutes
MAKES: 4 main-dish servings

1½ pounds small red potatoes, each cut into quarters

1 jumbo onion (1 pound), cut into 8 wedges

6 teaspoons olive oil

¾ teaspoon salt

¼ teaspoon coarsely ground black pepper

4 medium chicken breast halves, skin removed

2 tablespoons honey mustard

1. Preheat oven to 450°F. In small roasting pan (13" by 9"), toss potatoes and onion with 4 teaspoons oil, salt, and pepper. Place pan on middle rack and roast 25 minutes.

2. Meanwhile, place chicken breast halves in separate small roasting pan (13" by 9"); coat chicken with 1 teaspoon oil. In cup, mix remaining 1 teaspoon oil with honey mustard; set aside.

3. After potatoes and onions have baked 25 minutes, remove pan from oven and carefully turn pieces with metal spatula. Return to oven, placing pan on lower oven rack. Place chicken on upper rack.

4. After chicken has baked 10 minutes, remove from oven and brush with honey mustard mixture. Continue baking chicken, along with potatoes and onions, 12 to 15 minutes longer, until juices run clear when thickest part of chicken is pierced with a knife and potatoes and onions are golden and tender. Serve hot.

EACH SERVING: About 380 calories (24 percent calories from fat), 31g protein, 44g carbohydrate, 10g total fat (1g saturated), 3g fiber, 66mg cholesterol, 630mg sodium

---

THE SKINNY ON POULTRY

The breast is the most tender part of the bird—and also the leanest. Consider everyone's favorite, chicken: A three-and-a-half-ounce portion of breast meat without skin has about 4 grams of fat. The same amount of skinless dark meat has about 10 grams of fat.

And, whether you're eating chicken, turkey, duck, or Cornish hen, keep in mind that removing poultry skin slashes the amount of fat almost in half. You may prefer, however, to cook poultry with the skin on to keep the moisture in. Then simply remove the skin before eating. The fat reduction is practically the same, but the cooked bird will be juicier and more flavorful.

Healthy Makeover Fried Chicken

The crunchy coating is what seals in the juices, giving traditional Southern fried chicken its finger-licking flavor. Too bad it also absorbs so much fat. By stripping the bird of its skin, baking instead of frying, and ditching the batter for panko crumbs, our crispy cheat carves off 240 calories and 22 grams of fat per serving.

ACTIVE TIME: 10 minutes
TOTAL TIME: 45 minutes plus marinating
MAKES: 4 main-dish servings

1½ cups buttermilk

½ teaspoon cayenne (ground red) pepper

¾ teaspoon salt

1 (3 pound) cut-up chicken (8 pieces), skin removed from all pieces except wings

1½ cups panko (Japanese-style) bread crumbs

1 teaspoon grated fresh lemon peel

1. In large zip-tight plastic bag, place buttermilk, cayenne, and salt; add chicken pieces, turning to coat. Seal bag, pressing out excess air. Refrigerate chicken at least 1 hour or preferably overnight, turning bag over once.

2. Preheat oven to 425°F. Spray 15½" by 10½" jelly-roll pan with nonstick spray. In large bowl, combine panko and lemon peel.

3. Remove chicken from marinade, shaking off excess. Discard marinade. Add chicken pieces, a few at a time, to panko mixture, turning to coat. Place chicken in prepared pan.

4. Bake 30 to 35 minutes or until coating is crisp and juices run clear when thickest part of chicken is pierced with tip of knife. For browner coating, after chicken is cooked, turn oven to broil. Broil chicken 5 to 6 inches from source of heat 1 to 2 minutes or until golden brown.

EACH SERVING: About 305 calories (27 percent calories from fat), 36g protein, 16g carbohydrate, 9g total fat (3g saturated), 1g fiber, 101mg cholesterol, 370mg sodium ♥

Turkey Shepherd's Pie

Here's a good way to use up those Thanksgiving leftovers: a turkey-meat filling topped with leftover mashed potatoes. Although the canned chicken broth called for here works well, the dish is even better if you use the turkey carcass to make a flavorful homemade turkey broth.

ACTIVE TIME: 30 minutes
TOTAL TIME: 1 hour

MAKES: 4 main-dish servings

1	tablespoon olive oil
2	carrots, peeled and finely chopped
1	onion, finely chopped
1	celery stalk, finely chopped
2	cups mashed potatoes
¾	cup milk
2	tablespoons all-purpose flour
1	cup canned or homemade chicken broth (page 57) or turkey broth
8	ounces cooked turkey meat, cut into bite-size pieces (2 cups)
1	cup frozen peas
¼	teaspoon salt
⅛	teaspoon coarsely ground black pepper
pinch dried thyme	

1. In 5- to 6-quart Dutch oven, heat oil over medium heat. Add carrots, onion, and celery; cook until vegetables are tender and lightly browned, about 15 minutes.

2. Meanwhile, in small bowl, stir mashed potatoes with ¼ cup milk until combined.

3. Preheat oven to 450°F. In cup, with fork, mix flour with broth and remaining ½ cup milk until blended. Pour broth mixture into Dutch oven with vegetables. Cook over high heat, stirring often, until mixture boils and thickens slightly. Boil 1 minute. Reduce heat to medium; add turkey, frozen peas, salt, pepper, and thyme; heat through.

4. Place four 1½-cup ramekins or soufflé dishes on 15½" by 10½" jelly-roll pan for easier handling. Spoon warm turkey mixture into ramekins; top with potato mixture. Bake until hot, bubbly, and potatoes are lightly browned, 30 minutes.

EACH SERVING: About 320 calories (28 percent calories from fat), 25g protein, 33g carbohydrate, 10g total fat (3g saturated), 3g fiber, 54mg cholesterol, 615mg sodium 🍲

Chicken and Apple Meat Loaves

Easy to prepare chicken meat loaves spiced with fennel seeds, parsley, and brushed with an apple jelly and mustard sauce make for a scrumptious and calorie-saving main dish.

ACTIVE TIME: 25 minutes
TOTAL TIME: 1 hour

MAKES: 4 main-dish servings

1	slice whole wheat bread
¼	cup low-fat (1%) milk
4	medium Golden Delicious apples
1	pound ground dark-meat chicken
½	cup finely chopped onion
¼	cup packed fresh flat-leaf parsley leaves, finely chopped
1	large egg, lightly beaten
1½	teaspoons fennel seeds
½	teaspoon salt
½	teaspoon ground black pepper
1	tablespoon vegetable oil
¼	cup apple jelly
1	tablespoon Dijon mustard with seeds

Green beans for serving (optional)

1. Preheat oven to 450°F. In food processor with knife blade attached, pulse bread into fine crumbs. Transfer to large bowl and stir in milk; let crumbs soak. Meanwhile, grate half of 1 apple on large holes of box grater. Cut remaining apple half and remaining 3 apples into wedges, removing and discarding cores; set aside.

2. To bowl with crumbs, add chicken, onion, parsley, egg, grated apple, ½ teaspoon fennel seeds, salt, and pepper. With hands, mix until well combined. Divide mixture into 4 equal pieces. On 18" by 12" jelly-roll pan, form each piece into 4 ½" by 2 ½" loaf, spacing loaves 3 inches apart.

3. In large bowl, toss apples, oil, and remaining 1 teaspoon fennel seeds until well combined; scatter in even layer around meat loaves. Roast 10 minutes.

4. Meanwhile, stir together apple jelly and mustard until well blended. Brush or spoon thick layer of mixture onto meat loaves. Roast 10 minutes or until tops are browned and temperature on meat thermometer inserted into center of meat loaves reaches 165°F. Transfer apples and meat loaves to serving plates. Serve with green beans, if you like.

EACH SERVING: About 380 calories (26 percent calories from fat), 27g protein, 44g carbohydrate, 11g total fat (2g saturated), 6g fiber, 145mg cholesterol, 515mg sodium ⊕ ⬚

5

Beef, Pork, Veal & Lamb

If you're trying to cut back on red meat to lower your intake of saturated fat and cholesterol, you're not alone. The good news: You don't have to eliminate beef, pork, or even veal and lamb from your diet altogether (unless your doctor prescribes it). Simply focus on lean cuts of meat, like flank steak and pork tenderloin, and explore low-fat cooking methods, from grilling to roasting. We've provided lots of flavorful recipes—many rounded out with wholesome veggies and grains—so fire up your grill or preheat that oven. It's time to enjoy a little meat.

If you love steak and chops, our steak-and-pepper-filled fajitas, flank steak sandwiches, and rosemary lamb chops and allow you to indulge. See also "The Skinny on Grilled Meat" (page 103) for other lean cuts you can sink your teeth into. Or heat up a skillet and stir-fry slices of lean beef or pork with mixed vegetables; our orange-flavored pork and asparagus stir-fry is a winner.

We also offer low-maintenance slow-cooking roasts that make it easy for you to get a hot, home-cooked meal on the dinner table. Try our sweet and savory pork, which gets its sweetness from prunes and its salt from olives and capers, or our simple soy-honey roast tenderloin—just toss some sweet potatoes into the pot and you have a meal.

For some Mediterranean flair, try our Italian-inspired osso buco or Greek-style lamb kabobs with salad slaw.

Soy-Honey Pork with Sweet Potatoes (recipe page 107)

Pastrami-Spiced Flank Steak Sandwiches

Pastrami, a popular New York City deli item, probably came to us via the Romanians, who prepared many of their meats by rubbing them with aromatic spices and then smoking them. Although our pastrami isn't smoked, it is similarly coated with spices. Serve it on sliced rye with a side of coleslaw, deli style.

ACTIVE TIME: 15 minutes
TOTAL TIME: 30 minutes plus marinating

MAKES: 6 main-dish servings

1   tablespoon coriander seeds
1   tablespoon paprika
1   tablespoon cracked black pepper
2   teaspoons ground ginger
1½ teaspoons salt
1   teaspoon sugar
½   teaspoon crushed red pepper
3   garlic cloves, crushed with garlic press
1   beef flank steak (about 1½ pounds), well trimmed
12 slices rye bread
    deli-style mustard

1. In mortar with pestle or in zip-tight plastic bag with rolling pin, crush coriander seeds. In cup, mix coriander, paprika, black pepper, ginger, salt, sugar, and crushed red pepper.

2. Rub garlic on both sides of steak, then pat with spice mixture. Place steak in large zip-tight plastic bag; seal bag, pressing out excess air. Place bag on plate; refrigerate at least 2 hours or up to 24 hours.

3. Prepare outdoor grill for direct grilling over medium heat.

4. Remove steak from bag. Place steak on hot grill rack over medium heat and grill, turning once, 13 to 15 minutes for medium-rare or until desired doneness.

5. Place bread slices on grill rack over medium heat and toast, without turning, just until grill marks appear on underside of bread.

6. Transfer steak to cutting board and let stand 10 minutes to allow juices to set for easier slicing. Thinly slice steak across the grain and serve mounded on grilled rye bread with mustard alongside.

EACH SERVING: About 380 calories (28 percent calories from fat), 33g protein, 35g carbohydrate, 12g total fat (4g saturated), 3g fiber, 47mg cholesterol, 1,015mg sodium

TIP: *Crushing whole spices in a mortar with a pestle releases their flavorful oils, which makes the steak even tastier.*

Steak and Pepper Fajitas

Arrange the meat and condiments in pretty dishes and let each person make his own.

ACTIVE TIME: 10 minutes
TOTAL TIME: 30 minutes
MAKES: 4 main-dish servings

1	beef top round steak, 1 inch thick (¾ pound), well trimmed
1	jar (8 ounces) medium-hot chunky salsa
1	tablespoon light corn-oil spread (56% to 60% fat)
1	red onion, thinly sliced
1	green pepper, thinly sliced
1	red pepper, thinly sliced
2	tablespoons chopped fresh cilantro leaves
8	(6-inch) low-fat flour tortillas, warmed as label directs
1	container (8 ounces) fat-free sour cream
8	ounces fat-free sharp Cheddar cheese, shredded (2 cups)

chile peppers, lime wedges, and cilantro sprigs for garnish

1. Preheat broiler. Place steak on rack in broiling pan; spread ¼ cup salsa on top. Place pan in broiler at closest position to source of heat; broil steak 8 minutes. Turn steak over and spread ¼ cup salsa on top; broil 8 minutes longer for medium-rare or until desired doneness.

2. Meanwhile, in nonstick 12-inch skillet, melt corn-oil spread over medium heat. Add red onion, green pepper, and red pepper; cook until vegetables are tender-crisp. Stir in chopped cilantro. Spoon mixture into serving bowl.

3. Slice steak crosswise into thin slices. Serve steak with pepper mixture, tortillas, sour cream, shredded cheese, and remaining salsa. Garnish with chile peppers, lime wedges, and cilantro.

EACH SERVING: About 450 calories (14 percent calories from fat), 45g protein, 55g carbohydrate, 7g total fat (1g saturated), 6g fiber, 51mg cholesterol, 1,060mg sodium ♥ ⊕

THE SKINNY ON GRILLED MEAT

Grilling lends mouthwatering flavor to even the leanest cuts of meat. Try these options the next time you fire up your grill.

+ **BEEF:** Look for round or loin (eye or top round, tenderloin, or flank steak).
+ **PORK:** Choose loin or leg (tenderloin, loin, or sirloin chops).
+ **LAMB:** The leanest cuts are loin chops, boneless leg shank halves, or leg and shoulder cubes for kabobs.

+ **VEAL:** Get cutlets from leg or loin chops.

All of these cuts are 185 calories or less and have just 3 to 9 grams of fat per trimmed, cooked 3-ounce serving. When selecting meat, *rib* is the clue to high fat; so is *ground*—except if specifically labeled *90 percent lean* or higher. If you're craving burgers, preparing turkey or chicken patties is a smart, low-fat alternative. See "The Ground Roundup," page 69, for details.

Steak and Oven Fries

While the potatoes are in the oven, you can pan-fry the steak, make the red-wine-and-shallot sauce, and even whip up a salad and dressing. This dish pairs nicely with a simple salad such as romaine tossed with a vinaigrette.

ACTIVE TIME: 15 minutes
TOTAL TIME: 40 minutes
MAKES: 4 main-dish servings

Oven Fries (page 135)

1	beef flank steak (1 pound)
¼	teaspoon coarsely ground black pepper
2	teaspoons olive oil
1	large shallot, finely chopped
½	cup dry red wine
½	cup canned or homemade chicken broth (page 57)
2	tablespoons chopped fresh parsley

1. Prepare Oven Fries.

2. Meanwhile, pat steak dry with paper towels; sprinkle with pepper on both sides. Heat non-stick 12-inch skillet over medium heat until hot. Add steak and cook 7 minutes per side, turning over once, for medium-rare, or until desired doneness. Transfer steak to cutting board; keep warm.

3. To drippings in skillet, add olive oil; heat over medium heat. Add shallot and cook, stirring occasionally, until golden, about 2 minutes. Increase heat to medium-high. Add wine and broth; heat to boiling. Cook 3 to 4 minutes. Stir in parsley.

4. To serve, holding knife blade almost parallel to cutting surface, slice steak crosswise into thin slices. Spoon red-wine sauce over steak slices and serve with Oven Fries.

EACH SERVING WITH OVEN FRIES: About 390 calories (25 percent calories from fat), 31g protein, 40g carbohydrate, 11g total fat (4g saturated), 4g fiber, 46mg cholesterol, 455mg sodium ♥

COOKING WITH WINE

Wine adds fat-free flavor and body to quick pan sauces, stews, and poached fruit desserts. Because the success of any dish is determined by the quality of its ingredients, it is important to cook with good wine. Avoid the cooking wines sold in supermarkets; they're high in salt and low in flavor. Instead, consider using the leftovers from a bottle of wine served the night before or some of the wine you'll serve with the dish.

Beef Eye Round au Jus

Roast some herbed new potatoes while you prepare the beef. And for the tenderest results, do not roast this cut to more than medium-rare.

ACTIVE TIME: 30 minutes
TOTAL TIME: 1 hour 40 minutes
MAKES: 12 main-dish servings

1½ teaspoons salt
½ teaspoon dried thyme
¼ teaspoon ground black pepper
1 beef eye round roast (4 ½ pounds), trimmed
2 tablespoons olive oil
1 bag (16 ounces) carrots, peeled and cut into 2" by ¼" matchstick strips
1 pound leeks (3 medium), white and light green parts only, cut into 2" by ¼" matchstick strips
4 garlic cloves, thinly sliced
1¼ cups dry red wine
½ cup water
1 bay leaf

1. Preheat oven to 450°F. In small bowl, combine salt, thyme, and pepper; use to rub on roast. In 12-inch skillet, heat oil over medium-high heat until very hot. Add beef and cook until browned on all sides, about 10 minutes. Transfer beef to nonreactive medium roasting pan (14" by 10").

2. Add carrots, leeks, and garlic to skillet and cook, stirring occasionally, until carrots are tender, about 7 minutes. Arrange vegetable mixture around beef.

3. Roast beef 25 minutes. Add wine, water, and bay leaf to roasting pan. Turn oven control to 325°F and roast until meat thermometer inserted in center of roast reaches 140°F, about 45 minutes longer. Internal temperature of meat will rise to 145°F (medium) upon standing. Or roast until desired doneness. Remove and discard bay leaf.

4. When roast is done, transfer to warm large platter and let stand 15 minutes to set juices for easier slicing. To serve, cut roast into thin slices and serve with vegetables.

EACH SERVING: About 230 calories (28 percent calories from fat), 33g protein, 6g carbohydrate, 8g total fat (2g saturated), 1g fiber, 76mg cholesterol, 358mg sodium ♥

Pork Roast with Salsa Verde

Tomatillos are the main ingredient in salsa verde (green sauce). They bring a bright hint of lemon to this slow-cooker dish.

ACTIVE TIME: 10 minutes
SLOW-COOK TIME: 8 hours on Low or 5 hours on High
MAKES: 8 main-dish servings

1	large bunch cilantro
3	garlic cloves, sliced
2	pounds small red potatoes (about 8), cut into quarters
1	bone-in pork-shoulder roast (about 3 pounds), well trimmed
1	jar (16 to 18 ounces) salsa verde

1. From bunch of cilantro, remove and set aside 15 large sprigs. Remove enough leaves from remaining cilantro to equal ½ cup, loosely packed. Refrigerate leaves for garnish.

2. In 4½- to 6-quart slow-cooker pot, combine cilantro sprigs, garlic, and potatoes. Place pork on top of potato mixture. Pour salsa over and around pork. Cover slow cooker with lid and cook as manufacturer directs on Low 8 to 10 hours or on High 5 to 5½ hours.

3. Transfer pork to cutting board and slice. Transfer pork and potatoes to warm deep platter. Skim and discard fat and cilantro from cooking liquid. Spoon cooking liquid over pork and potatoes. Sprinkle reserved cilantro over pork.

EACH SERVING: About 300 calories (27 percent calories from fat), 25g protein, 27g carbohydrate, 9g total fat (3g saturated), 2g fiber, 79mg cholesterol, 295mg sodium ♥ ▢

Sweet and Savory Pork

Salty olives and capers interplay with sweet prunes to create a mouthwatering sauce.

ACTIVE TIME: 15 minutes
TOTAL TIME: 25 minutes
MAKES: 4 main-dish servings

1	pork tenderloin (1 pound), cut crosswise into 1-inch-thick slices, patted dry
2	tablespoons brown sugar
3	garlic cloves, crushed with garlic press
¾	teaspoon salt
¼	teaspoon ground black pepper
2	teaspoons olive oil
½	cup dry white wine
2	tablespoons red wine vinegar
1	teaspoon cornstarch
¼	teaspoon dried oregano
½	cup pitted prunes, coarsely chopped
¼	cup pitted green olives, coarsely chopped
2	tablespoons capers, drained

1. On waxed paper, combine brown sugar, garlic, salt, and pepper; use to coat pork.

2. In nonstick 12-inch skillet, heat oil over medium heat until hot. Add pork and cook until slices are lightly browned and lose their pink color throughout, about 3 minutes per side. Transfer pork to plate.

3. In cup, blend wine, vinegar, cornstarch, and oregano. Stir cornstarch mixture into skillet. Heat to boiling, stirring. Return pork to skillet. Add prunes, olives, and capers; heat through.

EACH SERVING: About 270 calories (23 percent calories from fat), 25g protein, 22g carbohydrate, 7g total fat (2g saturated), 2g fiber, 74mg cholesterol, 892mg sodium ◔

Soy-Honey Pork with Sweet Potatoes

Honey-soy glaze unites sweet potatoes and pork tenderloin for a very tasty meal. Let the hot oven do the work for you and enjoy your hassle-free dinner in only 40 minutes. For photo, see page 100.

ACTIVE TIME: 15 minutes
TOTAL TIME: 40 minutes
MAKES: 4 main-dish servings

¼	cup reduced-sodium soy sauce
2	tablespoons hoisin sauce
2	tablespoons honey
1	tablespoon rice vinegar
1	teaspoon grated, peeled fresh ginger
2	garlic cloves, crushed with press
1	whole pork tenderloin (1¼ pounds)
1½	pounds sweet potatoes
1	tablespoon vegetable oil
¼	teaspoon salt
⅛	teaspoon ground black pepper
2	green onions, cut into slivers

1. Preheat oven to 475°F. In small bowl, whisk soy sauce, hoisin, honey, vinegar, ginger, and half of garlic until well blended. Pour into gallon-size zip-tight plastic bag. Add pork; seal bag and turn until pork is well coated. Set aside.

2. Meanwhile, peel sweet potatoes. Cut each into ½-inch-thick rounds. In large bowl, combine oil and remaining garlic. Add sweet potatoes, salt, and pepper. Toss until well coated.

3. Transfer pork from marinade to center of 18″ by 12″ jelly-roll pan, shaking off any excess marinade into bag. Tuck tapered ends under pork to ensure even cooking. Arrange sweet potato rounds in single layer on pan around pork. Roast 10 minutes.

4. Meanwhile, transfer marinade to 2-quart saucepan. Heat to boiling over medium-high heat. Boil 3 minutes or until thickened and syrupy. Transfer half of marinade to small serving bowl; set aside. Turn sweet potatoes and pork over. Brush remaining marinade on pork. Roast 10 to 15 minutes longer or until temperature on meat thermometer inserted into thickest part of pork registers 155°F and sweet potatoes are browned. Cover pork loosely with foil and let stand 5 minutes.

5. Cut pork into ½-inch-thick slices.

6. Transfer pork and sweet potatoes to large platter. Garnish with green onions and serve with reserved marinade.

EACH SERVING: About 430 calories (19 percent total fat), 44g protein, 45g carbohydrate, 9g total fat (2g saturated), 4g fiber, 103mg cholesterol, 875mg sodium

Orange Pork and Asparagus Stir-Fry

Slices of lean pork tenderloin are quickly cooked with fresh asparagus and juicy orange pieces. For photo, see page 6.

ACTIVE TIME: 20 minutes
TOTAL TIME: 25 minutes

MAKES: 4 main-dish servings

2	navel oranges
1	teaspoon olive oil
1	pork tenderloin (about ¾ pound), trimmed and thinly sliced diagonally
¾	teaspoon salt
¼	teaspoon ground black pepper
1½	pounds thin asparagus, trimmed and each stalk cut crosswise in half
1	garlic clove, crushed with garlic press
¼	cup water

1. From 1 orange, grate 1 teaspoon peel and squeeze ¼ cup juice. Remove peel and white pith from remaining orange. Cut orange into ¼-inch-thick slices; cut each slice into quarters.

2. In nonstick 12-inch skillet, heat ½ teaspoon oil over medium heat until hot. Add half the pork, and sprinkle with ¼ teaspoon salt and ⅛ teaspoon pepper; cook, stirring frequently (stir-frying), until pork just loses its pink color, 2 minutes. Transfer pork to plate. Repeat with remaining pork, again using ½ teaspoon oil, ¼ teaspoon salt, and remaining ⅛ teaspoon pepper. Transfer pork to same plate.

3. To the same skillet, add asparagus, garlic, grated orange peel, remaining ¼ teaspoon salt, and water; cover and cook, stirring occasionally, until asparagus is tender-crisp, about 3 minutes. Return pork to skillet. Add reserved orange juice and orange pieces; heat through, stirring often.

EACH SERVING: About 165 calories (22 percent calories from fat), 24g protein, 8g carbohydrate, 4g total fat (1g saturated), 2g fiber, 50mg cholesterol, 495mg sodium

EAT YOUR ASPARAGUS

Fresh asparagus is a springtime treat not to be missed. It's a great source of folic acid, which protects against heart disease and birth defects, so women of child-bearing years should add it to their menu. Enjoy it with rich salmon, or steam up a handful (it takes less than 10 minutes), sprinkle lightly with salt or a little grated Parmesan cheese, and enjoy. At 3 calories a spear, you can afford to eat a whole bunch.

Sesame Pork Stir-Fry

So gingery good—and this one-dish meal is only 375 calories per serving.

ACTIVE TIME: 20 minutes
TOTAL TIME: 40 minutes
MAKES: 4 main-dish servings

Aromatic Brown Rice (page 132)

1	cup loosely packed watercress leaves, coarsely chopped
1	pork tenderloin (12 ounces), trimmed and thinly sliced
2	tablespoons soy sauce
1	tablespoon minced, peeled fresh ginger
1	teaspoon Asian sesame oil
1	garlic clove, crushed with garlic press
¾	cup canned or homemade chicken broth (page 57)
1¼	teaspoons cornstarch
2	teaspoons olive oil
3	carrots, peeled and cut into 2" by ¼" matchstick strips
1	red pepper, cut into ¼-inch-wide strips
1	tablespoon water
1	medium zucchini (about 8 ounces), cut into 2" by ¼" matchstick strips

1. Prepare Aromatic Brown Rice. Stir in watercress and keep warm.

2. Meanwhile, in medium bowl, toss pork, soy sauce, ginger, sesame oil, and garlic. In cup, mix broth and cornstarch; set aside.

3. In nonstick 12-inch skillet, heat 1 teaspoon olive oil over medium heat until hot. Add carrots and red pepper; cook, stirring frequently (stir-frying), until lightly browned, about 5 minutes. Add water and stir-fry until vegetables are tender-crisp, 3 to 5 minutes longer. Transfer to bowl.

4. In same skillet, heat remaining 1 teaspoon olive oil. Add zucchini; stir-fry until tender-crisp, about 3 minutes. Transfer zucchini to bowl with other vegetables.

5. To same skillet, add pork mixture and stir-fry until pork just loses its pink color. Stir cornstarch mixture; add to pork. Stir in vegetables; heat to boiling. Boil until sauce thickens, 1 minute. Serve stir-fry with watercress rice.

EACH SERVING: About 375 calories (24 percent calories from fat), 23g protein, 48g carbohydrate, 10g total fat (2g saturated), 3g fiber, 56mg cholesterol, 975mg sodium

Osso Buco
with Gremolata

This aromatic recipe from northern Italy is a wonderful choice for company. A risotto is the traditional accompaniment, or for a lower-calorie meal, pair the veal with broccoli rabe tossed with a little balsamic vinegar.

ACTIVE TIME: 40 minutes
TOTAL TIME: 2 hours 40 minutes
MAKES: 4 main-dish servings

4	meaty veal shank cross cuts (osso buco), each about 2 inches thick (1 pound total)
½	teaspoon salt
¼	teaspoon ground black pepper
1	tablespoon olive oil
2	onions, chopped
3	carrots, peeled and chopped
2	stalks celery, chopped
4	garlic cloves, finely chopped
1	can (14½ to 16 ounces) tomatoes in puree
1	cup dry white wine
1	cup canned or homemade chicken broth (see page 57)
1	bay leaf
2	tablespoons chopped fresh parsley
½	teaspoon freshly grated lemon peel

1. Preheat oven to 350°F. Sprinkle shanks with salt and pepper. In nonreactive 5-quart Dutch oven, heat oil over medium-high heat until very hot. Add shanks and cook until browned on both sides, about 10 minutes, transferring shanks to plate as they are browned.

2. Add onions to Dutch oven and cook over medium heat, stirring occasionally, until slightly browned, about 5 minutes. Add carrots, celery, and three-fourths of garlic and cook 2 minutes longer.

3. Return veal to Dutch oven. Stir in tomatoes with their puree, wine, broth, and bay leaf; heat to boiling over high heat. Cover and place in oven. Bake until veal is tender when pierced with fork, about 2 hours.

4. Meanwhile, prepare gremolata: In small bowl, mix parsley, lemon peel, and remaining garlic. Cover and refrigerate until ready to serve.

5. Transfer veal to platter. Heat sauce in Dutch oven to boiling over high heat; boil until it has reduced to 4 cups, about 10 minutes. Pour sauce over veal and sprinkle with gremolata.

EACH SERVING: About 375 calories (17 percent calories from fat), 53g protein, 20g carbohydrate, 8g total fat (2g saturated), 4g fiber, 183mg cholesterol, 874mg sodium

Glazed Rosemary Lamb Chops

These rosemary-scented lamb chops are broiled with an apple-jelly and balsamic-vinegar glaze. Keep this glaze in mind for pork, too.

ACTIVE TIME: 10 minutes
TOTAL TIME: 20 minutes

MAKES: 4 main-dish servings

8   lamb loin chops, 1 inch thick (4 ounces each)
1   large garlic clove, cut in half
2   teaspoons chopped fresh rosemary or ½ teaspoon dried rosemary, crumbled
¼   teaspoon salt
¼   teaspoon coarsely ground black pepper
¼   cup apple jelly
1   tablespoon balsamic vinegar

1. Preheat broiler as manufacturer directs. Rub both sides of each lamb chop with garlic. Sprinkle lamb with rosemary, salt, and pepper. In cup, combine apple jelly and balsamic vinegar.

2. Place chops on rack in broiling pan. With pan at closest position to source of heat; broil chops 4 minutes. Brush chops with half of apple-jelly mixture; broil 1 minute. Turn chops and broil 4 minutes longer. Brush chops with remaining jelly mixture and broil 1 minute longer for medium-rare or until desired doneness.

3. Transfer lamb to warm platter. Skim and discard fat from drippings in pan. Serve chops with pan juices or drizzle lamb with additional balsamic vinegar.

EACH SERVING: About 240 calories (30 percent calories from fat), 26g protein, 14g carbohydrate, 8g total fat (3g saturated), 0g fiber, 82mg cholesterol, 223mg sodium ♥ ♥

Lamb Kabobs and Salad Slaw

This is a delicious meal in one.

ACTIVE TIME: 40 minutes
TOTAL TIME: 50 minutes
MAKES: 4 main-dish servings

1	pound boneless leg of lamb, from shank
⅓	cup chili sauce
2	tablespoons teriyaki sauce
¼	head red cabbage
1	head romaine lettuce
1	bunch green onions
1	large navel orange
¼	cup orange juice
2	tablespoons low-fat mayonnaise
1	tablespoon cider vinegar
1	teaspoon prepared mustard
¼	teaspoon cracked black pepper
⅛	teaspoon salt
4	(12-inch) metal skewers

1. Trim all fat from lamb. Cut lamb into 12 chunks. In medium bowl, mix lamb, chili sauce, and teriyaki sauce until lamb is coated; set aside.

2. Thinly slice cabbage; discard any tough ribs. Cut romaine crosswise into ¼-inch-thick ribbons. Cut green onions into 2-inch pieces. Cut orange in half; cut each half into 3 wedges; cut each wedge crosswise in half.

3. In large bowl, stir orange juice, mayonnaise, vinegar, mustard, pepper, and salt until blended. Add cabbage and lettuce; toss salad slaw until dressing is evenly distributed.

4. Prepare outdoor grill for direct grilling over medium heat.

5. On skewers, alternately thread lamb chunks, green-onion pieces, and orange pieces. Place skewers on hot grill rack over medium heat. Cook lamb 10 to 12 minutes for medium-rare or until desired doneness, turning once.

6. Transfer skewers to platter. Serve kabobs with salad slaw and orange wedges.

EACH SERVING: About 265 calories (30 percent calories from fat), 28g protein, 20g carbohydrate, 9g total fat (3g saturated), 7g fiber, 74mg cholesterol, 810mg sodium ♥

EAT YOUR CITRUS

Looking for some vitamin C? Head to the citrus section of your supermarket! Go beyond the traditional oranges and try diminutive clementines, garnet-fleshed blood oranges, giant yellow and pink grapefruit, and bite-size kumquats—all are rich in vitamin C. On average, a single piece of citrus fruit also contains 3 grams of fiber and only about 50 calories. While a glass of fresh-squeezed OJ is pretty sweet in the morning, you'll miss out on that good fiber if you drink your citrus instead of eating it.

6

Meatless Mains

Looking to incorporate more grains and greens into your family's diet? We have the perfect solution: Go vegetarian a couple nights a week. Here, we provide so many tasty options, your kids will be looking forward to Meatless Mondays in no time.

Start with familiar favorites. Serve our hearty black bean burgers with a side of oven-fried potatoes (page 135) or our crunchy carrot coleslaw (page 38).

When you're feeling more adventurous, our farro risotto and wheat-berry pilaf recipes provide hearty meals with a complete balance of protein, healthy grains, and plenty of vegetables. (And if you omit the Parmesan, you can serve these dishes to your vegan friends, too.)

And, of course, we have not forgotten the noodles. Our ratatouille rigatoni, sprinkled with just a little cheese, has the power to entice even the most adamant eggplant detractors. Other options include our family-style lasagna (it's brimming with healthy veggies) or mac and cheese, which features whole-grain pasta and tomato slices for a more wholesome take on everybody's go-to comfort food.

Ratatouille Rigatoni (recipe page 123)

Black-Bean Burgers

Spicy cumin and coriander flavor these healthy meat-free black-bean burgers.

ACTIVE TIME: 15 minutes
TOTAL TIME: 20 minutes
MAKES: 4 main-dish servings

¼   cup dried bread crumbs

¼   teaspoon ground cumin

¼   teaspoon ground coriander

2   cans (15 ounces each) low-sodium black beans, rinsed and drained, or 3 cups cooked black beans

4   tablespoons light mayonnaise

¼   teaspoon salt

¼   teaspoon ground black pepper

2   large stalks celery, finely chopped

1   chipotle chile in adobo, finely chopped

4   green-leaf lettuce leaves

4   whole-wheat hamburger buns, toasted

4   slices ripe tomato

1. In food processor with knife blade attached, pulse bread crumbs, cumin, coriander, two-thirds of beans, 2 tablespoons mayonnaise, salt, and pepper until well blended. Transfer to large bowl. Stir in celery and remaining whole beans until well combined. Divide into 4 portions and shape into patties.

2. Lightly coat nonstick 12-inch skillet with nonstick cooking spray. Heat on medium 1 minute, then add patties. Cook 10 to 12 minutes or until browned on both sides, turning once.

3. Meanwhile, in small bowl, combine chipotle chile and remaining 2 tablespoons mayonnaise until well mixed. Place 1 lettuce leaf on bottom of each bun; top with patty, then tomato slice. Divide chipotle mayonnaise among burgers and replace tops of buns to serve.

EACH SERVING: About 370 calories (19 percent calories from fat), 18g protein, 59g carbohydrate, 8g total fat (1g saturated), 14g fiber, 5mg cholesterol, 725mg sodium

Farro Risotto with Butternut Squash

The firm, chewy texture of farro resembles Arborio rice but boasts the nutritional characteristics of spelt. Italians have enjoyed this grain since the days of the Roman Empire.

ACTIVE TIME: 20 minutes
TOTAL TIME: 55 minutes

MAKES: 4 main-dish servings

1	tablespoon olive oil
1	small onion, finely chopped
½	teaspoon salt
¼	teaspoon ground black pepper
1½	cups farro (emmer wheat)
½	cup dry white wine
1¼	cups water
1	can (14½ ounces) vegetable broth or 1¾ cups homemade (page 56)
⅛	teaspoon dried thyme
⅛	teaspoon dried rosemary, crushed
1	butternut squash (2 pounds), peeled and cut into ½-inch pieces
½	cup freshly grated Parmesan cheese, plus additional for serving
¼	cup loosely packed fresh parsley leaves, chopped

1. In deep nonstick 12-inch skillet, heat oil over medium heat until hot. Add onion, salt, and pepper, and cook 5 to 7 minutes or until onion is tender and lightly browned. Add farro and cook 2 to 3 minutes or until lightly browned, stirring constantly. Add wine and cook about 1 minute or until absorbed.

2. To farro mixture in skillet, add water, broth, thyme, and rosemary; cover skillet and heat to boiling over high heat. Stir in squash; reduce heat to medium-low. Cover and simmer about 20 minutes longer or until farro is just tender (mixture will still be soupy).

3. Uncover and cook 1 to 2 minutes longer over high heat, stirring constantly, until most liquid is absorbed. Remove skillet from heat and stir in Parmesan and parsley. Serve with additional Parmesan, if you like.

EACH SERVING: About 415 calories (20 percent calories from fat), 16g protein, 74g carbohydrate, 9g total fat (3g saturated), 6g fiber, 8mg cholesterol, 925mg sodium ☻

BROWN RICE RISOTTO WITH BUTTERNUT SQUASH: Prepare recipe as above, substituting *1½ cups regular long-grain brown rice* for farro. In step 2, add *2½ cups water* and cook rice 45 minutes (instead of 20 minutes) on medium-low heat, once pot is covered and simmering.

EACH SERVING: About 445 calories (18 percent calories from fat), 13g protein, 80g carbohydrate, 9g total fat (3g saturated), 6g fiber, 8mg cholesterol, 930mg sodium ☻

Wheat-Berry Pilaf with Green Beans

Make this tasty veggie-flecked combination of brown rice and wheat berries the centerpiece of a vegetarian meal.

ACTIVE TIME: 30 minutes
TOTAL TIME: 1 hour, 30 minutes
MAKES: 4 main-dish or 8 side-dish servings

1	cup wheat berries (whole-wheat kernels)
4	cups water
½	cup long-grain brown rice
3	teaspoons olive oil
4	carrots, peeled and cut into ½-inch dice
2	stalks celery, cut into ½-inch dice
1	large onion (12 ounces), cut into ½-inch dice
1	can (14½ ounces) vegetable broth or 1¾ cups homemade (page 56)
8	ounces green beans, trimmed and cut into 1½-inch pieces
¾	teaspoon salt
½	teaspoon freshly grated orange peel
¼	teaspoon coarsely ground black pepper
¼	teaspoon dried thyme
¾	cup dried cranberries

1. In 3-quart saucepan, heat wheat berries and water to boiling over high heat. Reduce heat to low; cover and simmer until wheat berries are firm to the bite but tender enough to eat, about 50 minutes; drain and set aside.

2. Meanwhile, in 2-quart saucepan, prepare brown rice as label directs, but do not add butter or salt.

GET YOUR GRAINS: WHEAT BERRIES

Whole wheat is a nutritional powerhouse, containing thirteen B vitamins, vitamin E, protein, and essential fatty acids. Wheat berries are unmilled kernels of wheat; they are chewy with a pleasant nutty taste that makes them a great choice for salads. The coarsely crushed kernels of wheat are sold as cracked wheat. Because the kernels have been split open, cracked wheat cooks more quickly than wheat berries, so use it when you need to get whole-grain goodness fast!

3. While wheat berries and brown rice are cooking, in deep 12-inch skillet, heat 2 teaspoons oil over medium heat until hot. Add carrots and celery; cook until almost tender, about 10 minutes, stirring occasionally. Add onion and remaining 1 teaspoon oil; cook until vegetables are lightly browned, 12 to 15 minutes longer, stirring occasionally.

4. Increase heat to high; add broth, green beans, salt, orange peel, pepper, and thyme, and heat to boiling. Reduce heat to medium-high; cook until green beans are just tender, about 5 minutes, stirring often.

5. Add cranberries, wheat berries, and brown rice to skillet; stir to combine.

EACH MAIN-DISH SERVING: About 425 calories (13 percent calories from fat), 14g protein, 84g carbohydrate, 6g total fat (1g saturated), 12g fiber, 0mg cholesterol, 790mg sodium

Whole-Wheat Penne Genovese

An onion-flecked white bean sauté adds heft to this fresh and healthy pesto pasta dish, making it light yet satisfying.

ACTIVE TIME: 15 minutes
TOTAL TIME: 30 minutes
MAKES: 6 main-dish servings

12   ounces whole-wheat penne or rotini
1½ cups packed fresh basil leaves
1   garlic clove, peeled
3   tablespoons water
3   tablespoons extra-virgin olive oil
¼   teaspoon salt
¼   teaspoon ground black pepper
½   cup grated Parmesan cheese
1   small onion (4 to 6 ounces), chopped
1   can (15 to 19 ounces) white kidney beans (cannellini), rinsed and drained
1   pint grape tomatoes (red, yellow, and orange mix if available), cut into quarters

1. In large saucepot, cook pasta as label directs.

2. Meanwhile, make pesto: In food processor with knife blade attached, blend basil, garlic, water, 2 tablespoons oil, salt, and pepper until pureed, stopping processor occasionally and scraping bowl with rubber spatula. Add Parmesan; pulse to combine. Set aside.

3. In 12-inch skillet, heat remaining 1 tablespoon oil over medium heat until very hot; add onion and cook 5 to 7 minutes or until beginning to soften. Stir in white beans, and cook 5 minutes longer, stirring occasionally.

4. Reserve *¼ cup pasta cooking water*. Drain pasta and return to saucepot; stir in white bean mixture, pesto, tomatoes, and reserved cooking water. Toss to coat.

EACH SERVING: About 375 calories (24 percent calories from fat), 15g protein, 59g carbohydrate, 10g total fat (2g saturated), 9g fiber, 5mg cholesterol, 435mg sodium ♡ ♥ ✿

Family Vegetarian Lasagna

This low-cal lasagna is meat-free and loaded with veggies. It tastes great as a leftover, so you can make it over the weekend and serve it later in the week, on a busy night.

ACTIVE TIME: 25 minutes
TOTAL TIME: 1 hour 15 minutes

MAKES: 4 main-dish servings

2	zucchini or yellow summer squash, thinly sliced
2	teaspoons olive oil
¼	teaspoon salt
1	bunch Swiss chard, tough stems discarded, thinly sliced
1	small onion (4 to 6 ounces), finely chopped
2	garlic cloves, crushed with press
1	teaspoon fresh thyme leaves, chopped
1	pound plum tomatoes, cored and thinly sliced
4	no-boil lasagna noodles, rinsed with cold water
2	carrots, peeled and shredded
1	cup part-skim ricotta cheese
1	ounce provolone cheese, finely shredded (¼ cup)

1. Arrange one oven rack 4 inches from broiler heat source and place second rack in center. Preheat broiler.

2. In large bowl, toss zucchini with 1 teaspoon oil and ⅛ teaspoon salt. Arrange on 18″ by 12″ jelly-roll pan in single layer. Broil 6 minutes or until golden brown, turning over once. Set aside. Reset oven control to 425°F.

3. Rinse chard in cold water; drain, leaving some water clinging to leaves.

4. In 12-inch skillet, heat remaining 1 teaspoon oil over medium heat. Add onion and cook 3 minutes or until soft, stirring occasionally. Add chard, garlic, thyme, and remaining ⅛ teaspoon salt. Cook 6 to 7 minutes or until chard is very soft, stirring frequently. Remove from heat and set aside.

5. In 8-inch square baking dish, layer half of tomatoes, lasagna noodles, Swiss chard, shredded carrots, zucchini slices, and ricotta, in that order. Repeat layering once. Top with provolone. Cover with foil. (Lasagna can be prepared to this point and refrigerated overnight.) Bake 30 minutes, covered. (If refrigerated, bake 10 minutes longer.) Uncover and bake 20 minutes longer or until golden brown and bubbling.

EACH SERVING: About 275 calories (29 percent calories from fat), 16g protein, 33g carbohydrate, 9g total fat (5g saturated), 6g fiber, 29mg cholesterol, 541mg sodium ♨ 🍴

Healthy Makeover Macaroni and Cheese

Predictable: Our classic mac and cheese, with its 1¼ pounds of cheese, has 640 calories and 30 fat grams per serving. Surprising: Our revamped version, with reduced-fat cheese and low-fat milk, is still creamy and flavorful but has only 420 calories and 12 fat grams for the same serving size.

ACTIVE TIME: 15 minutes
TOTAL TIME: 30 minutes

MAKES: 4 main-dish servings

8	ounces whole-wheat rotini pasta (2½ cups)
4	teaspoons cornstarch
2	cups low-fat (1%) milk
½	teaspoon Dijon mustard
¼	teaspoon salt
¼	teaspoon ground black pepper
4	ounces reduced-fat (2%) pasteurized process cheese spread, cut into ½-inch cubes
2	ounces extra-sharp Cheddar cheese, shredded (½ cup)
⅓	cup freshly grated Pecorino-Romano cheese
2	tablespoons plain dried bread crumbs
1	medium tomato, thinly sliced

1. Cook pasta as label directs.

2. Meanwhile, in 2-quart saucepan, whisk cornstarch into milk; heat to boiling over medium heat, whisking occasionally. Boil 1 minute. Remove saucepan from heat; whisk in mustard, salt, and pepper. Stir in pasteurized process cheese, Cheddar, and ¼ cup Romano. (Cheese does not need to melt completely.) In small bowl, combine bread crumbs with remaining Romano.

3. Preheat broiler. Spray shallow 1½-quart broiler-safe baking dish with nonstick cooking spray.

4. When pasta is done, drain and return to saucepot. Stir cheese sauce into pasta; spoon into prepared baking dish. Arrange tomato slices on top; sprinkle with crumb mixture.

5. Place baking dish in broiler about 6 inches from source of heat. Broil macaroni mixture 2 to 3 minutes or until top is lightly browned. Let macaroni and cheese stand 5 minutes to set slightly for easier serving.

EACH SERVING: About 420 calories (26 percent calories from fat), 23g protein, 59g carbohydrate, 12g total fat (7g saturated), 5g fiber, 37mg cholesterol, 920mg sodium ♥ ❤ ▦

Ratatouille Rigatoni

Traditional vegetables for French ratatouille (eggplant, yellow summer squash, peppers and onions) are roasted and turned into a healthy vegetarian sauce for rigatoni pasta. For photo, see page 114.

ACTIVE TIME: 15 minutes
TOTAL TIME: 1 hour

MAKES: 6 main-dish servings

1	large eggplant (15 ounces), trimmed and cut into ½-inch cubes
1	small onion (6 to 8 ounces), cut into ½-inch pieces
3	tablespoons extra-virgin olive oil
½	teaspoon salt
½	teaspoon ground black pepper
1	package (16 ounces) rigatoni pasta
2	yellow summer squash, cut into ½-inch pieces
1	medium red pepper (4 to 6 ounces), cut into ½-inch pieces
1	can (14½ ounces) crushed tomatoes
1	garlic clove, crushed with press
½	cup fresh basil leaves, very thinly sliced
½	cup freshly grated Parmesan cheese

1. Preheat oven to 450°F. In 18" by 12" jelly-roll pan, combine eggplant, onion, 2 tablespoons oil, ¼ teaspoon salt, and ¼ teaspoon black pepper until well mixed. Spread in even layer. Roast vegetables 15 minutes.

2. Meanwhile, in saucepot, cook pasta as label directs. To pan with eggplant, add squash, red pepper, remaining 1 tablespoon oil and remaining ¼ teaspoon each salt and black pepper. Stir gently until well mixed, then spread vegetables in even layer. Roast 25 to 30 minutes longer or until vegetables are very tender.

3. When pasta is done, drain and set aside. In same saucepot, heat tomatoes with their juice and garlic to boiling over medium-high heat; cook 4 minutes or until slightly thickened. Remove from heat; add pasta and roasted vegetables and basil; toss together until well combined.

4. Divide pasta and vegetable mixture among warm serving bowls. Sprinkle with grated Parmesan to serve.

EACH SERVING: About 445 calories (22 percent calories from fat), 16g protein, 72g carbohydrate, 11g total fat (3g saturated), 7g fiber, 7mg cholesterol, 670mg sodium 🌱 🍲

EAT YOUR EGGPLANT

It's worth the effort to learn to like eggplant: That bitter taste comes, in part, from chlorogenic acid, which helps prevent cancer and can also keep heart-threatening plaque from building up. What's more, lab studies show that eating eggplant lowers LDL cholesterol and helps artery walls relax, which can cut your risk for high blood pressure. To mellow eggplant's flavor, try grilling or slow-roasting it. (Salting it and letting it stand for 30 minutes also helps draw out some of the bitterness. Rinse off the salt before proceeding with your recipe.)

Side Dishes

We've provided recipes for all our favorite light and healthy mains; now it's time to share some simple, healthy sides to pair with them. Hearty recipes for whole grains and many low-cal, low-fat ways to prepare everyone's favorite—the potato—are all included. And we've also tackled green vegetables that you or your family members may be reluctant to eat by adding irresistible flavors.

If you're looking for an easy way to prepare veggies, try microwave-steaming (see "Easy Microwave-Steamed Vegetables," page 130). We provide a selection of flavorful low-fat dressings to top off green beans, broccoli, yellow squash, zucchini, spinach, Swiss chard, collard greens, asparagus, cauliflower, eggplant, and new potatoes (see "Low-Fat Ways to Dress Your Veggies," page 129).

If your main dish doesn't include grains, serve up our brown rice pilaf or prepare our brown rice and cranberry stuffing. And, as mentioned above, we have not forgotten the potatoes: Try them herb-roasted in a foil packet, smashed, or oven-baked, so you can enjoy French "fries" without all the fat.

Mashed Sweet Potatoes (recipe page 134)

Tarragon Peas and Pearl Onions

Fresh tarragon adds a perky licorice flavor to these lightly cooked peas and pearl onions.

ACTIVE TIME: 6 minutes
TOTAL TIME: 16 minutes

MAKES: 8 side-dish servings

1	tablespoon margarine or butter
1	bag (16 ounces) frozen pearl onions
1	bag (16 ounces) frozen peas
¼	cup water
½	teaspoon salt
¼	teaspoon ground black pepper
1	tablespoon chopped fresh tarragon leaves

1. In nonstick 12-inch skillet, heat margarine over medium heat until melted. Add frozen pearl onions and cook 7 to 9 minutes or until browned.

2. Add frozen peas, water, salt, and pepper to skillet; stir to combine. Cover and cook 3 to 4 minutes longer or until onions and peas are tender. Stir tarragon into vegetables and spoon into serving bowl.

EACH SERVING: About 75 calories (20 percent calories from fat), 3g protein, 12g carbohydrate, 2g total fat (0g saturated), 4g fiber, 0mg cholesterol, 202mg sodium ♥ ♥

Sesame Green Beans

These Asian-inspired green beans are delicious served hot or at room temperature.

ACTIVE TIME: 15 minutes
TOTAL TIME: 20 minutes

MAKES: 4 side-dish servings

1	teaspoon salt
1	pound green beans, trimmed
1	tablespoon soy sauce
½	teaspoon Asian sesame oil
1½	teaspoons minced, peeled fresh ginger or ¾ teaspoon ground ginger
1½	teaspoons sesame seeds, toasted

1. In 4-quart saucepan, combine *7 cups water* and salt; heat to boiling over high heat. Add green beans; heat to boiling. Cover and cook until just tender-crisp, 6 to 8 minutes. Drain; return green beans to saucepan.

2. Add soy sauce, sesame oil, and ginger to green beans in saucepan. Cook over low heat, stirring occasionally, until flavors have blended, about 3 minutes. Transfer to serving bowl and sprinkle with sesame seeds.

EACH SERVING: About 45 calories (20 percent calories from fat), 2g protein, 8g carbohydrate, 1g total fat (0g saturated), 3g fiber, 0mg cholesterol, 553mg sodium ♥ ▤

Green Beans with Caramelized Onions

Caramelized onions make everything better. And this green-bean side dish—a lighter take on a beloved holiday casserole—is no exception.

ACTIVE TIME: 30 minutes
TOTAL TIME: 1 hour 10 minutes
MAKES: 14 cups or 16 side-dish servings

3	pounds green beans, trimmed
1½	pounds red onions (about 3 medium), each cut in half, then sliced
3	tablespoons margarine or butter
1	tablespoon fresh thyme leaves, chopped
1½	teaspoons salt
½	teaspoon ground black pepper

1. Fill large bowl with *ice water* to cool beans quickly after cooking; set aside. Heat 6- to 8-quart saucepot of *salted water* to boiling over high heat. Add beans in 2 batches and cook each batch 4 minutes or until beans are tender-crisp, making sure water returns to boiling before adding each batch of beans. With slotted spoon or sieve, transfer beans to bowl of ice water. Drain beans thoroughly.

2. In nonstick 12-inch skillet, combine onions, margarine, thyme, salt, and pepper. Cook over medium heat 15 minutes or until onions start to brown, stirring occasionally. Reduce heat to medium-low and cook 5 to 7 minutes longer or until onions turn dark brown, stirring frequently. Stir beans into onion mixture; heat through before serving.

EACH SERVING: About 60 calories (30 percent calories from fat), 2g protein, 9g carbohydrate, 2g total fat (0g saturated), 3g fiber, 0mg cholesterol, 250mg sodium ♥ ▣

TIP: *If you'd like to make this dish ahead of time, up to two days in advance, blanch, cool, and drain beans. Cook onion mixture and cool. Refrigerate each component separately in sealed plastic bags. To reheat, toss beans and onion mixture into 4-quart microwave-safe glass bowl. Microwave on High about 8 minutes, stirring halfway through heating.*

LOW-FAT WAYS TO DRESS YOUR VEGGIES

Boost the flavor—without loading on the fat—with these simple alternatives to classic butter, cheese, and cream sauces.

FOR GREEN BEANS OR BROCCOLI

+ Thin orange marmalade with a little water; whisk in some ground ginger and heat over low. Stir sauce into hot green beans or broccoli flowerets.
+ Blend prepared horseradish, Dijon mustard, and light mayonnaise; drizzle over steamed green beans.
+ Whisk together seasoned rice vinegar, soy sauce, and grated fresh ginger to taste. Use as a dipping sauce for tender-crisp broccoli.

FOR YELLOW SQUASH OR ZUCCHINI

+ Toast bread crumbs with chopped garlic in 1 teaspoon of olive oil. Sprinkle over steamed yellow squash along with some chopped parsley.
+ Flavor cooked zucchini with a dusting of freshly grated Parmesan cheese (a little goes a long way) and cracked black pepper.

FOR DARK, LEAFY GREENS (SPINACH, SWISS CHARD, COLLARDS)

+ Sauté minced garlic and a pinch of crushed red pepper in 1 teaspoon of olive oil until fragrant. Add fresh spinach or Swiss chard to pan and cook until wilted.
+ Slice a piece of Canadian bacon (it's surprisingly low fat) into thin strips and cook in a nonstick skillet until crisp. Toss with boiled collard greens or steamed spinach.
+ Add a handful of yellow raisins to steamed bitter greens, such as Swiss chard.

FOR ASPARAGUS OR CAULIFLOWER

+ Prepare a mock hollandaise by mixing light mayonnaise with Dijon mustard, fresh lemon juice, and a pinch of ground pepper. Drizzle the cool sauce over steamed cauliflower, broccoli, or—the classic hollandaise partner—asparagus spears.
+ Chop some mango chutney (available in the gourmet or international section of most supermarkets) and toss it with steamed cauliflower or asparagus.

FOR EGGPLANT

+ Heat chopped fresh tomato with crushed fennel seeds in a skillet until hot. Spoon over baked or broiled eggplant slices.

FOR NEW POTATOES

+ Toss chopped mixed fresh herbs (such as basil, mint, rosemary, or oregano) and grated lemon zest with boiled new potato halves. Season with salt to taste.

Mixed Pea Pod Stir-Fry

This sweet and tender-crisp medley celebrates the glorious flavor of fresh green vegetables.

ACTIVE TIME: 15 minutes
TOTAL TIME: 16 minutes
MAKES: 4 side-dish servings

1	teaspoon salt
8	ounces green beans, trimmed
2	teaspoons vegetable oil
4	ounces snow peas, trimmed and strings removed
4	ounces sugar snap peas, trimmed and strings removed
1	garlic clove, finely chopped
1	tablespoon soy sauce

1. In 12-inch skillet, combine *4 cups water* and salt; heat to boiling over high heat. Add green beans and cook 3 minutes. Drain; wipe skillet dry with paper towels.

2. In same skillet, heat oil over high heat. Add green beans and cook, stirring frequently (stir-frying), until they begin to brown, 2 to 3 minutes. Add snow peas, sugar snap peas, and garlic; stir-fry until snow peas and sugar snap peas are tender-crisp, about 1 minute longer. Stir in soy sauce and remove from heat.

EACH SERVING: About 65 calories (28 percent calories from fat), 3g protein, 8g carbohydrate, 2g total fat (0g saturated), 3g fiber, 0mg cholesterol, 844mg sodium ●

EASY MICROWAVE-STEAMED VEGETABLES

Want tasty vegetables fast? Follow these simple instructions and the cook-time chart opposite to microwave-steam perfect veggies every time. In microwave cooking, vegetables retain more vitamins and minerals because they cook quickly with little or no water. And greasing a bowl or dish with oil or butter isn't necessary, since the microwave's moist heat prevents sticking.

In a covered, microwave-safe dish, cook one pound vegetables (or amount specified opposite) with ¼ cup water on High until tender, stirring once halfway through cooking time. Take care not to overcook; the finished veggies should be crisp and brightly colored, never mushy. Season with salt and pepper and serve.

VEGETABLE	MINUTES TO COOK
Asparagus	4 to 6
Beans, green or yellow wax	4 to 7
Beets, whole (remove the greens)	10 to 14
Bell peppers, cut into strips	5 to 7
Broccoli flowerets	5 to 6
Carrots, peeled and sliced	5 to 8
Cauliflower flowerets	5 to 6
Peas, shelled (1 cup)	4 to 5
Spinach (10 ounces)	30 to 90 seconds
Zucchini or yellow squash, sliced	4 to 7

Aromatic Brown Rice

Think of rice as a blank canvas that you can add any number of flavorings to for your own taste creation. Below is a basic recipe for brown rice, followed by three very different variations.

ACTIVE TIME: 5 minutes
TOTAL TIME: 25 minutes

MAKES: 4 side-dish servings

1	cup long-grain brown rice
1	cup canned or homemade chicken or vegetable broth (pages 56–57)
¾	cup water
¼	teaspoon salt

In a medium saucepan, combine rice, broth, water, and salt and bring to boiling, uncovered, over high heat. Cover and simmer over low heat until rice is tender and liquid is absorbed, 18 to 20 minutes.

EACH SERVING: About 175 calories (10 percent calories from fat), 4g protein, 36g carbohydrate, 2g total fat (Og saturated), 3g fiber, Omg cholesterol, 295mg sodium ✔ 🍱

ORANGE-CILANTRO BROWN RICE: After rice has cooked, stir in *2 tablespoons chopped fresh cilantro* and *½ teaspoon freshly grated orange peel.*

EACH SERVING: About 175 calories (5 percent calories from fat), 4g protein, 37g carbohydrate, 1g total fat (Og saturated), 3g fiber, 3mg cholesterol, 295mg sodium ✔ 🍱

ASIAN BROWN RICE: Omit salt when cooking rice. After rice has cooked, stir in *2 green onions,* chopped, *2 teaspoons soy sauce,* and *¼ teaspoon Asian sesame oil.*

EACH SERVING: About 180 calories (5 percent calories from fat), 4g protein, 38g carbohydrate, 1g total fat (Og saturated), 3g fiber, 3mg cholesterol, 380mg sodium ✔ 🍱

LEMON-PARSLEY BROWN RICE: After rice has cooked, stir in *2 tablespoons chopped fresh parsley* and *1 teaspoon freshly grated lemon peel.*

EACH SERVING: About 175 calories (5 percent calories from fat), 4g protein, 37g carbohydrate, 1g total fat (Og saturated), 3g fiber, 3mg cholesterol, 295mg sodium ✔ 🍱

Brown Rice and Vegetable Pilaf

Add beans, rotisserie chicken, or shrimp to this versatile pilaf and dinner is served.

ACTIVE TIME: 15 minutes
TOTAL TIME: 1 hour 25 minutes
MAKES: 6 side-dish servings

1	tablespoon olive or vegetable oil
1	medium onion, finely chopped
1	stalk celery, finely chopped
1	package (8 ounces) mushrooms, trimmed and sliced
1	garlic clove, finely chopped
1	cup long-grain brown rice
2¼	cups water
2	carrots, peeled and chopped
1¼	teaspoons salt
⅛	teaspoon dried thyme
⅛	teaspoon ground black pepper

pinch dried sage

1. In 10-inch skillet, heat oil over medium heat. Add onion and celery; cook until onion is tender, about 5 minutes, stirring frequently. Stir in mushrooms; increase heat to medium-high and cook until mushrooms begin to brown and liquid has evaporated. Stir in garlic. Add rice; cook, stirring, 30 seconds. Stir in water, carrots, salt, thyme, pepper, and sage; heat to boiling.

2. Reduce heat; cover and simmer until rice is tender and all liquid has been absorbed, about 45 minutes. Fluff with fork.

EACH SERVING: About 165 calories (16 percent calories from fat), 4g protein, 31g carbohydrate, 3g total fat (0g saturated), 3g fiber, 0mg cholesterol, 503mg sodium

Brown Rice and Cranberry Stuffing

Here's a flavorful low-fat alternative to ordinary bread stuffing.

ACTIVE TIME: 45 minutes
TOTAL TIME: 2 hours
MAKES: 11 cups or 22 side-dish servings

2	tablespoons olive oil
3	medium carrots, peeled and cut into ½-inch pieces
2	medium fennel bulbs, trimmed and cut into ¼-inch pieces
2	stalks celery, cut into ¼-inch pieces
1	medium onion, chopped
3	cups long-grain brown rice
1	can (14½ ounces) chicken broth or 1¾ cups homemade (page 57)
¾	cup dried cranberries
1¾	teaspoons salt
½	teaspoon dried thyme
¼	teaspoon coarsely ground black pepper
4½	cups water

1. Preheat oven to 325°F.

2. In 12-inch skillet, heat oil over medium heat until hot. Add carrots, fennel, celery, and onion and cook until vegetables are tender and lightly browned, about 20 minutes, stirring frequently.

3. Stir in rice, broth, cranberries, salt, thyme, pepper, and water. Cover and heat to boiling. Pour rice mixture into 13" by 9" baking dish; cover with foil and bake until liquid is absorbed and rice is tender, about 1 hour 15 minutes.

EACH SERVING: About 135 calories (13 percent calories from fat), 3g protein, 26g carbohydrate, 2g total fat (0g saturated), 3g fiber, 0mg cholesterol, 265mg sodium

Honeyed Hot Fruit Salad

A few turns on the grill transform fresh fruit into a sumptuous side. For photo, see page 8.

ACTIVE TIME: 15 minutes
TOTAL TIME: 25 minutes

MAKES: 6 servings

½	cup honey
1	tablespoon fresh lemon juice
¼	cup loosely packed fresh mint leaves, thinly sliced
1	medium pineapple, cut lengthwise into 6 wedges, with leaves attached
2	large bananas, peeled and each cut diagonally into thirds
3	medium plums, each cut in half and pitted
2	medium nectarines or peaches, each cut into quarters and pitted

1. Prepare outdoor grill for direct grilling over medium heat.

2. In cup, stir honey, lemon juice, and 1 tablespoon sliced mint.

3. With tongs, place fruit pieces on hot grill rack over medium heat and grill, turning fruit occasionally and brushing it with honey mixture during last 3 minutes of cooking, until browned and tender, 10 to 15 minutes.

4. To serve, arrange grilled fruit on large platter; drizzle with any remaining honey mixture. Sprinkle with remaining mint.

EACH SERVING: About 215 calories (4 percent calories from fat), 2g protein, 55g carbohydrate, 1g total fat (0g saturated), 5g fiber, 0mg cholesterol, 5mg sodium ● ●

Mashed Sweet Potatoes

You don't have to wait until the holidays to enjoy this delectable side dish. A few tablespoons of soy sauce add a salty, earthy flavor to our rendition of this favorite. For photo, see page 124.

ACTIVE TIME: 10 minutes
TOTAL TIME: 20 minutes

MAKES: 12 side-dish servings

4	pounds sweet potatoes (5 medium), peeled and cut into 1½-inch chunks
4	tablespoons butter or margarine
3	tablespoons soy sauce
1	green onion, thinly sliced

1. In 5- or 6-quart saucepot, place sweet potatoes and enough *water* to cover; heat to boiling over high heat. Reduce heat to medium-low; cover and cook 10 to 12 minutes or until potatoes are tender. Drain well and set potatoes aside.

2. In same saucepot, melt butter over medium heat. Remove saucepot from heat; add soy sauce and potatoes. With potato masher, mash potatoes until almost smooth. Transfer to serving bowl and sprinkle with green onion.

EACH SERVING: About 150 calories (24 percent calories from fat), 2g protein, 27g carbohydrate, 4g total fat (1g saturated), 3g fiber, 0mg cholesterol, 310mg sodium ● ♥ ▣

Herb-Roasted Potatoes

Potato chunks tossed with parsley and butter cook into tender morsels when foil-wrapped. For photo, see page 12.

ACTIVE TIME: 15 minutes
TOTAL TIME: 45 minutes

MAKES: 6 side-dish servings

2   tablespoons butter or margarine
1   tablespoon chopped fresh parsley
½   teaspoon freshly grated lemon peel
½   teaspoon salt
⅛   teaspoon coarsely ground black pepper
1½ pounds small red potatoes, each cut in half

1. Preheat oven to 450°F. In 3-quart saucepan, melt butter with parsley, lemon peel, salt, and pepper over medium-low heat. Remove saucepan from heat; add potatoes and toss well to coat.

2. Place potato mixture in center of 24" by 18" sheet of heavy-duty foil. Fold edges over and pinch to seal tightly.

3. Place package in jelly-roll pan and bake until potatoes are tender when potatoes are pierced (through foil) with knife, about 30 minutes.

EACH SERVING: About 125 calories (29 percent calories from fat), 2g protein, 20g carbohydrate, 4g total fat (2g saturated), 1g fiber, 10mg cholesterol, 241mg sodium ♥

Oven Fries

You won't miss the fat in these hand-cut "fries." They bake beautifully in a jelly-roll pan with a spritz of nonstick cooking spray and a sprinkle of salt and pepper.

ACTIVE TIME: 10 minutes
TOTAL TIME: 30 minutes

MAKES: 4 side-dish servings

nonstick cooking spray
3   medium baking potatoes (8 ounces each)
½   teaspoon salt
¼   teaspoon coarsely ground black pepper

1. Preheat oven to 500°F. Spray two 15½" by 10½" jelly-roll pans or 2 large cookie sheets with nonstick cooking spray.

2. Scrub unpeeled potatoes well, but do not peel. Cut each potato lengthwise in half. With each potato half cut side down, cut lengthwise into ¼-inch-thick slices. Place potatoes in medium bowl and toss with salt and pepper.

3. Divide potato slices between pans and spray potatoes with nonstick cooking spray. Roast potatoes until tender and lightly browned, about 20 minutes, rotating pans between upper and lower racks halfway through roasting time.

EACH SERVING: About 130 calories (7 percent calories from fat), 4g protein, 28g carbohydrate, 1g total fat (0g saturated), 3g fiber, 0mg cholesterol, 280mg sodium ♥ ♥

ROSEMARY AND GARLIC OVEN FRIES: Prepare Oven Fries as above, but in step 3 add *½ teaspoon dried rosemary, crumbled,* and *2 garlic cloves, crushed with garlic press.*

Metric Equivalents

The recipes in this book use the standard United States method for measuring liquid and dry or solid ingredients (teaspoons, tablespoons, and cups). The information in these charts is provided to help cooks outside the U.S. successfully use these recipes. All equivalents are approximate.

METRIC EQUIVALENTS FOR DIFFERENT TYPES OF INGREDIENTS

A standard cup measure of a dry or solid ingredient will vary in weight depending on the type of ingredient. A standard cup of liquid is the same volume for any type of liquid. Use the following chart when converting standard cup measures to grams (weight) or milliliters (volume).

Standard Cup	Fine Powder (e.g., flour)	Grain (e.g., rice)	Granular (e.g., sugar)	Liquid Solids (e.g., butter)	Liquid (e.g., milk)
1	140 g	150 g	190 g	200 g	240 ml
³/₄	105 g	113 g	143 g	150 g	180 ml
²/₃	93 g	100 g	125 g	133 g	160 ml
¹/₂	70 g	75 g	95 g	100 g	120 ml
¹/₃	47 g	50 g	63 g	67 g	80 ml
¹/₄	35 g	38 g	48 g	50 g	60 ml
¹/₈	18 g	19 g	24 g	25 g	30 ml

USEFUL EQUIVALENTS FOR COOKING / OVEN TEMPERATURES

	Fahrenheit	Celsius	Gas Mark
Freeze water	32° F	0° C	
Room temperature	68° F	20° C	
Boil water	212° F	100° C	
Bake	325° F	160° C	3
	350° F	180° C	4
	375° F	190° C	5
	400° F	200° C	6
	425° F	220° C	7
	450° F	230° C	8
Broil			Grill

USEFUL EQUIVALENTS FOR LIQUID INGREDIENTS BY VOLUME

¹/₄ tsp	=			1 ml
¹/₂ tsp	=			2 ml
1 tsp	=			5 ml
3 tsp	=	1 tblsp	= ¹/₂ fl oz	15 ml
2 tblsp	=	¹/₈ cup	= 1 fl oz	30 ml
4 tblsp	=	¹/₄ cup	= 2 fl oz	60 ml
5 ¹/₃ tblsp	=	¹/₃ cup	= 3 fl oz	80 ml
8 tblsp	=	¹/₂ cup	= 4 fl oz	120 ml
10 ²/₃ tblsp	=	²/₃ cup	= 5 fl oz	160 ml
12 tblsp	=	³/₄ cup	= 6 fl oz	180 ml
16 tblsp	=	1 cup	= 8 fl oz	240 ml
1 pt	=	2 cups	= 16 fl oz	480 ml
1 qt	=	4 cups	= 32 fl oz	960 ml
			33 fl oz	1000 ml

USEFUL EQUIVALENTS FOR DRY INGREDIENTS BY WEIGHT

(To convert ounces to grams, multiply the number of ounces by 30.)

1 oz	=	¹/₁₆ lb	=	30 g
4 oz	=	¹/₄ lb	=	120 g
8 oz	=	¹/₂ lb	=	240 g
12 oz	=	³/₄ lb	=	360 g
16 oz	=	1 lb	=	480 g

USEFUL EQUIVALENTS FOR LENGTH

(To convert inches to centimeters, multiply the number of inches by 2.5.)

1 in	=			2.5 cm	
6 in	= ¹/₂ ft	=		15 cm	
12 in	= 1 ft	=		30 cm	
36 in	= 3 ft	= 1 yd	=	90 cm	
40 in	=			100 cm	= 1 m

Photography Credits

Front Cover, Spine: Kate Mathis

Back Cover: Kate Sears

Antonio Achilleos: 2, 74

James Baigrie: 10, 11, 22, 30, 45 (right), 65, 83, 124, 126

Monica Buck: 15

Tara Donne: 21, 54, 88, 91, 95, 122

Brian Hagiwara: 20, 32, 43, 62, 122, 84, 102

iStockphoto: AleaImage, 13; Ursula Alter, 98; Hilary Brodey, 61; Olga Brovina, 94; Kelly Cline, 129; Melanie DeFaziom 108; Le Do, 45 (left); Only Fabrizio, 41; Trevor Fisher, 105; Floortje, 132; Juanmonino, 76; Kryczka, 53; Chris Leachman, 35; Joanna Pecha, 31; Robert Pears, 56; Viktor Pravdica, 112; Vitalina Rybakova, 80 (left); Ken Rygh, 73; James Steidl, 18; Nikolay Suslov, 36; Jarek Szymanski, 28; Alasdair Thomson, 51; Yin Yang, 27

Frances Janisch: 97

Yunhee Kim: 29

Rita Maas: 12, 131

Kate Mathis: 24, 49, 50, 66, 79, 117, 121

Con Poulos: 70, 99, 100, 120

Alan Richardson: 6, 8, 39, 68

Kate Sears: 5, 67, 80 (right), 86, 92, 114

Shutterstock: 109; Fortish, 64; MdN, 55; Olga Miltsova, 107; Yuliya Rusyayeva, 60; Yasonya, 46

Ann Stratton: 128

Studio D: Philip Friedman, 9

Mark Thomas: 111

Index

Index of Recipes by Icon

This index makes it easy to search recipes by category, including 30 minutes or less, heart healthy, high fiber, and make ahead.

🌐 HIGH FIBER

Want to get more fill-you-up fiber into your diet? Incorporate the following high fiber dishes into your regular repertoire. Each of these recipes contains 5 grams or more fiber per serving.

🍲 MAKE AHEAD

For convenience, you can make all (or a portion) of these recipes ahead of time. The individual recipes indicate which steps you can complete ahead of time, or indicate how long you can refrigerate or freeze the completed dish.

The Good Housekeeping
Triple-Test Promise

At *Good Housekeeping*, we want to make sure that every recipe we print works in any oven, with any brand of ingredient, no matter what. That's why, in our test kitchens at the **Good Housekeeping Research Institute**, we go all out: We test each recipe at least three times—and, often, several more times after that.

When a recipe is first developed, one member of our team prepares the dish and we judge it on these criteria: It must be **delicious, family-friendly, healthy,** and **easy to make**.

1   The recipe is then tested several more times to fine-tune the flavor and ease of preparation, always by the same team member, using the same equipment.

2   Next, another team member follows the recipe as written, **varying the brands of ingredients** and **kinds of equipment**. Even the types of stoves we use are changed.

3   A third team member repeats the whole process **using yet another set of equipment** and **alternative ingredients**. By the time the recipes appear on these pages, they are guaranteed to work in any kitchen, including yours. **We promise.**